British Origins of

American Colonists,

1629-1775

British Origins of

American Colonists,

1629-1775

William Dollarhide

Heritage Quest Genealogical Services, a division of AGLL, Inc.
Bountiful, Utah
1997

Published by Heritage Quest Genealogical Services, a division of AGLL, Inc., Bountiful, Utah

Printed in the United States of America

2002   2001   1999   1998   6   5   4   3   2

ISBN 1-877677-69-8

To Brad and Raeone Steuart.

They said I had to do this.

Contents

Maps

Preface

This book identifies the county origins of the main migration groups from the British Isles to the American colonies before the Revolutionary War. Four distinct migration groups are identified:

1. The **East Anglian Puritans** to New England, 1629-1640.

2. The **West Country Cavaliers** and their Servants to the Chesapeake, 1641-1675.

3. The **North Midland Quakers** to the Delaware Valley, 1675-1715.

4. The **British and Scottish borderers** (the so-called "Scotch-Irish") to the backwoods of the American colonies, 1717-1775.

These groups were not the very first colonies, but the ones that came after the first experiments in colonizing British North America. Clearly, these four waves of immigrants came in greater numbers and had greater success in establishing themselves in the New World. If an American today has a British ancestor who arrived during the colonial period, there is a very high chance that he was part of one of these four waves of migrations.

The goal of this book is to provide a genealogical researcher with guidelines that will aid in locating a British ancestral home. The guidelines assume that a researcher has no specific knowledge of the origins of his British immigrants. Much of the information about the origins of the four groups is based on estimated percentages, and necessarily, some generalizations. For example, the 21,000 Puritans who came to America during the Great Migration of 1629-1640 originated from nearly every county in England; but about half of them came from just three counties. In fact, a large percentage of each of the four groups came from specific cluster regions of the British Isles. So, even with such generalizations about their origins, it may be possible to have a starting point in British research with higher odds for success than taking a shotgun approach to research in the British Isles.

All four migration groups left their homes in the British Isles during a specific span of years, from an eleven year period for the Puritans, to a fifty-seven year span for the Scotch-Irish migration. Each group was a minority in Britain, either in their politics or their religious beliefs. Their history is one of social, political, and religious turmoil; and they believed their lives could be improved by moving to America. Most of the groups settled in specific cluster areas of colonial America. Therefore, if a researcher knows the first place an ancestor lived in America within an approximate time period, that information should provide a strong pointer to his British home within a limited number of counties. The maps in the book identify the locations where each group lived in Great Britain, as well as the places they settled in America.

Finding the Home of
a British Emigrant

A Needle
in a Haystack

There is a scientific method that can be used to find a needle in a haystack. First, see if you can determine where the needle most likely went into the haystack. With this information, you should have a starting point. Next, carefully remove the areas of the stack of hay the needle probably did not touch. The task becomes one of reducing the stack of hay to the smallest size possible. Now begin sifting and removing the pieces of straw one-by-one to find the needle. The smaller the stack of hay can be reduced in size, the better your chances will be to find the needle.

So, before jumping into a large haystack or making random searches in English county records, let's start by understanding where our ancestors from England may have lived just before their journey to America. In other words, let's reduce the size of the haystack. There were very specific groups that started the first colonies in America. And, it can be determined that certain counties of England supplied large groups of immigrants to America. By identifying the places in England where these groups lived, perhaps we can narrow down the number of counties where you need to search for evidence of your ancestor in England. To accomplish this process, you

must first know something about your immigrant ancestor in America. If you are able to determine where he came to live first and the approximate time period in which he arrived, then you have a good starting point.

Your British ancestor was probably not from the first permanent English colony in America, the Virginia Company, which began in Jamestown in 1607. Like most of the earliest colonies, the Jamestown settlement was made up mostly of men who died young and unmarried. For example, there are almost no descendants of the founders of the Jamestown colony in America. Of the 104 original settlers of Jamestown, only one is known to have had surviving descendants in America. His name was Robert Beheathland. The rest of the descendants of these men were born in England and remained there, although later generations may have migrated to America.[1]

After Jamestown, the most famous British settlement was New Plymouth, established in 1620 in Massachusetts and consisted of Pilgrims seeking religious freedom. The genealogies available to researchers outlining the descendants of the Mayflower and subsequent Pilgrim arrivals are well known and documented. If you can connect to an ancestor as one of the Pilgrims of New Plymouth Colony, your work will have been done for you already. But the Pilgrims

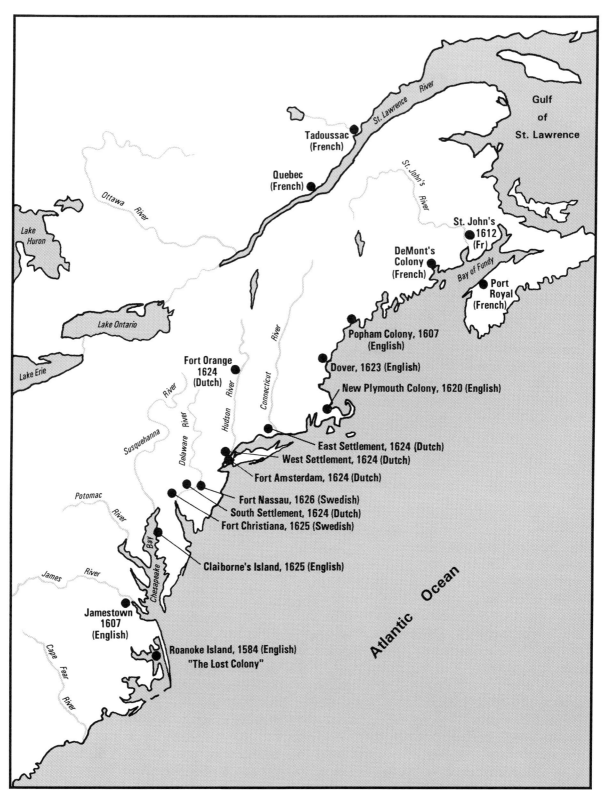

Atlantic Colonies, 1607-1626. The first American colonies were founded by small groups of settlers consisting mostly of men who died young and unmarried. It was after this period that larger and more organized groups were successful in planting settlements, beginning with the migration of the Puritans to New England in 1629.

were incorporated into the larger and more successful Massachusetts Bay Colony after only a few decades. Later generations of the original Pilgrims were overshadowed by the children of the Puritans, the dominant group of settlers in early Massachusetts.

After the early 17th Century experiments in colonizing North America, larger and better organized groups of settlers began arriving in the New World. The first of these large groups was the migration of Puritans to New England beginning in 1629. Since the numbers of settlers increased, the work of locating an ancestral home in the Britain Isles for an emigrant increases in difficulty. Without family stories or written sources that tell you the place where your ancestors lived, the work to locate an ancestral home in Britain may actually feel like trying to find a needle in a haystack.

Therefore, if we are to be successful in locating British records that reveal the names of our early immigrant ancestors, we need to employ the same techniques we use in finding the homes of our American ancestors. We need to first find the jurisdiction in which they lived. We know, for example, that locating the right county of residence in America is the key to finding records for an ancestor who lived there. With that knowledge, one can begin a systematic search of published county records that may reveal evidence of a family name.

American genealogical research is often keyed to the land a person owned. Land ownership in America before 1850 was as high as 90 percent of all adult white males. As a result, U.S. land records are nearly universal as finding tools. And, since real estate transactions are recorded at the county level in the U.S. for most states, indexes to deeds provide a excellent historic overview of the residents of a county in virtually every state. It is estimated that family researchers have a 90% chance of success for locating a place of residence for a person in the U.S. just by reading deed indexes, county-by-county, within any state. Another advantage to American research is the early Federal censuses taken since 1790 which frequently list the names of immigrants or their descendants. A census name index or a deed index acts as a valuable place-finding tool for further research in America.

British Place-finding Sources

Unlike American sources, land records as an effective tool for English research are mostly limited to an elite society of landlords. And, since nationwide census records in England which list names of people did not begin until 1841, they do not provide the names of emigrants to America during the colonial period. Locating the home of a person in 17th Century British records requires other general name lists that may help locate the county and then a parish within a county where that person lived. An English parish is the jurisdiction where vital statistics such as births, baptisms, marriages, deaths, and burials are recorded. If a name can be connected to just a few English counties, the job of searching parish records within each county becomes a task that is more easily accomplished.

There are some national sources for surnames in the British Isles. A few of them are identified below. Without knowing a specific location for a particular surname in Britain, for example, a search of one of these large name lists may reveal a location where a particular surname occurs. If nothing else, the name lists may show where a particular surname is most commonly found and perhaps narrow down the number of counties that need to be searched in more detail.

To use these name lists effectively, a researcher should have more than one name to help refine the task of finding a residence for a person. For example, if a researcher knows the surname of an Englishman and the maiden name of his wife, the work gets easier because you now have two surnames to link to a particular place. Additionally, researchers should find allied names, such as an ancestor's neighbors in America who, due to the fact that they lived near your ancestor, may have traveled with him from the same place in England. Adding more names for the search in these place-finding sources is a method of narrowing down the number of places where a certain group of surnames occur.

So, the first task in British research is to find a county where your ancestor's surname appears. Then, a search of each parish within that county is necessary. It is in the parish records where we can find confirmation of a person's residence in Great Britain. Fortunately, many of the parish records of the British Isles have been microfilmed and are available for research in this country through the Family History Library of The Church of Jesus Christ of Latter-day Saints and its many branches across the country. In addition, many of the parish registers available on microform are available at the Library of Congress in Washington, D.C. These can be obtained on inter-library loan at over 6,000 public libraries across the nation.

Here are some general place-finding sources for the British Isles. These are large name lists which can be used to locate a place in the British Isles where a certain surname may occur:

■ **Telephone Books and Directories.** A telephone book is a source for locating a name in a certain place. Even a current directory is valuable, which can confirm if a certain name still occurs in that place today. This is because descendants of your British families with the same surnames may still live in the same village, parish, or county. A selection of British phone books are available at many libraries in this country. Privately published nationwide phone directories on CD-ROM are also available for English places. (One is called *Brit-phone.*) These are also found in larger U.S. libraries.

■ **International Genealogical Index.**[TM] This is an outstanding tool that can be used in locating a British home. The International Genealogical Index (IGI) is available at the Family History Library in Salt Lake City and at more than 2,000 Family History Centers across the U.S. The IGI is a computerized index to surnames. It is divided by country. The British section contains over 30 million entries. Most of the entries were extracted from British parish records, especially baptisms and marriages. The IGI can be used to find a surname in a certain place in Britain, because it generally gives the precise county or parish location in Britain where a particular name was found. Even without knowing the relationship of a person listed in the IGI, it is useful to conduct this type of search. It may reduce the number of counties where a particular name occurs. To locate a Family History Center (FHC), use a phone directory to locate a Church of Jesus Christ of Latter-day Saints Chapel. Call and ask where the nearest FHC is located in your area. They are all open to the general public.

■ **Genealogical Research Directory** (GRD). This is an international directory in which genealogical researchers from around the world advertise the names of people they want to find. The directory lists ancestral names in alphabetical order, along with the names and addressess of the persons who submittted the names. The GRD is an annual publication with at least 150,000 name entries per year. Since 1980, the GRD has published over two million name entries. The GRD becomes a place-finding tool. If a particular person back in time is listed in the GRD, the place of that person's residence, birth, marriage, or death is also listed. Even if the name is not recognized as an ancestor, the connection of the name to a place, such as a parish or county of England, is of great value. The GRD is published in Australia and has submitters from countries all over the world. The current and back issues of the GRD can be found in larger U.S. libraries with genealogy sections. The American representative is Mrs. Jan Jennings, 3324 Crail Way, Glendale, CA 91206-1107. (E-mail: jxpfo4b@prodigy.com). A recent compilation of the past five years of GRD entries was made available as a single CD-ROM disk, containing over 500,-000 name entries listed in alphabetical order.

■ **British Isles Genealogical Register.** This is a compilation of names of interest to British genealogists published by the Federation of Family History Societies of England. Created in 1994, it lists over 300,000 names submitted by British genealogists over the past twenty years. Many of the names came from an earlier publication of the Society of Genealogists called the *National Genealogical Register* which was published annually for several years. It is now a microfilm publication and is available at the Family History Library in Salt Lake City and through inter-library loan at over 2,000 local Family History Centers. Since all entries are related to British names and places, it can be a useful tool in locating a place in the British Isles where a particular surname occurs. It may also connect an American researcher with a genealogist in the British Isles following the same surname.

■ **Boyd's Marriage Index.** This index to English marriage records was compiled by Percival Boyd, one of England's most acclaimed genealogists. It contains over seven million name entries taken from parish registers, bishops' transcripts, and marriage licenses. The index does not cover every county of England but is virtually complete for all marriages which occurred between 1538 and 1837 in all parishes within the city of London and the counties of Cambridgeshire, Cornwall, Cumberland, Derbyshire, Devonshire, Durham, Essex, Gloucestershire, Lancashire, Middlesex, Norfolk, Northumberland, Shropshire, Somerset, Suffolk, and Yorkshire. The printed county-wide volumes

of Boyd's Index are available in this country at the Family History Library in Salt Lake City. Microfilm versions are available on interlibrary loan at the many local Family History Centers across the U.S.

■ **Family Origin Name Survey** (FONS). This is a two-part computerized genealogical research database. The first part contains abstracts of all known surviving British record material from the period before 1600, with the exception of parish baptisms and marriages, 1538-1600 (which should eventually be covered by the International Genealogical Index). The **Pre-1600 Record Sources** include administrations, ancient deeds, assize rolls, bishops' registers, cartularies, charter rolls, courts baron, courts leet, curia regis rolls, ecclesiastical courts, eyre, feet of fines, fine rolls, heraldic visitations, hundred rolls, inquisitions, lay subsidies, liberate rolls, pipe rolls, poll taxes, proofs of age, star chamber, state papers, treaty rolls, and wills.

The second database, the **Non-Register Archives, 1600-1858** contains an archives of will abstracts, will lists, and other name lists such as poll books, land tax assessments, muster rolls, etc., for the period 1600 to 1858. In both databases, the information consists of abstracts of the original records, along with a name index to any person mentioned in any way. The two databanks were compiled from existing computer databases as well as manual indexes which have been computerized and incorporated into the system. They were originated as research sources specific to the study of the origins and distribution of surname groups in England from 1086 to 1858. Either database is an outstanding source for locating a surname, perhaps in an obscure record. The research will lead a genealogist to a particular county or parish location in which a surname occurs. This is a private database, and one must become a member of the organization to obtain access to it. For more information, contact the Family Origin Name Survey, The Strines, Leek, Staffordshire, ST13 8UL, England. A registration and life membership applies to each of the databases and costs $10.00 (in U.S. funds) for one membership, or $20.00 for both. Members can pre-pay for 5 to 100 entries for a surname search in either database. There is a fee of $5.00 per entry found in the database. As additional information is added to the databases, the FONS group will search for your surnames on a continuing basis until the pre-paid limit is reached. Additional searches can be added at any time in the future without paying the registration fee again.

✦ ✦ ✦ ✦ ✦ ✦

NOTES

1. William Thorndale, "Drew Pickayes (1564-1607), A Jamestown Founder", in *The American Genealogist,* Vol. 70, No. 3 (July 1995), page 129.

The East Anglian Puritans, 1629-1640

It was no accident that during an eleven year period 21,000 immigrants left England for the Massachusetts Bay Colony. This period was called the "Eleven Years Tyranny" of England, when King Charles I disbanded Parliament to rule England by himself and Archbishop William Laud purged the Anglican church of its Puritan members. It was also an era of economic depression, epidemic disease, and so many sufferings that John Winthrop said the land had become "weary of her Inhabitants, so as man which is most precious of all the Creatures, is here more vile and base than the earth they tread upon." [1]

During these eleven years, some 80,000 oppressed Puritans felt compelled to leave England. About a quarter of them went to the Netherlands and another quarter went to Ireland. Another quarter went to the West Indies islands of Barbados, Nevis, and St. Kitts. A fourth contingent came to America and founded the Massachusetts Bay Colony.

The first Puritans arrived in New England in 1629. The following year, there were seventeen shiploads of Puritans to America led by John Winthrop, often called the "Winthrop Fleet," with about 2,000 immigrants. This was the vanguard of a total of some 200 ships, each carrying about 100 passengers. This exodus continued to the year 1640. During that time, it was a busy ocean. In 1638 one immigrant aboard a ship bound for Boston Harbor sighted 13 ships also in midpassage to Massachusetts.

The Great Migration ended as suddenly as it had begun. A Civil War in England was the reason. In fact, some of the Massachusetts immigrants returned to England to fight in the war. Soon after the Great Migration, a period of unrest commenced in England in which both Charles I and Archbishop Laud were executed and in which Puritan Oliver Cromwell became England's "Lord Protector." Migrations of the scale of 1629-1640 did not return to Massachusetts again until the middle of the nineteenth century when Irish Catholics came in great numbers during the potato famine of Ireland.

In describing the Puritan migration to New England, historian David Hackett Fischer observed that "the immigrants who came to New England in the Great Migration became the breeding stock for America's Yankee population. They multiplied at a rapid rate, doubling every generation for 200 years. Their numbers increased to 100,000 by 1790 and to one million people by 1900, and an estimated sixteen million by 1988 — all descended from 21,000 English immigrants who came to Massachusetts in the period 1629 to 1640. The children of the great migration moved rapidly beyond the borders of Massachusetts. They occupied much of southern New England, including Connecticut and Rhode Island, eastern New Jersey, and northern New York. Their descendants migrated east to Maine and Nova

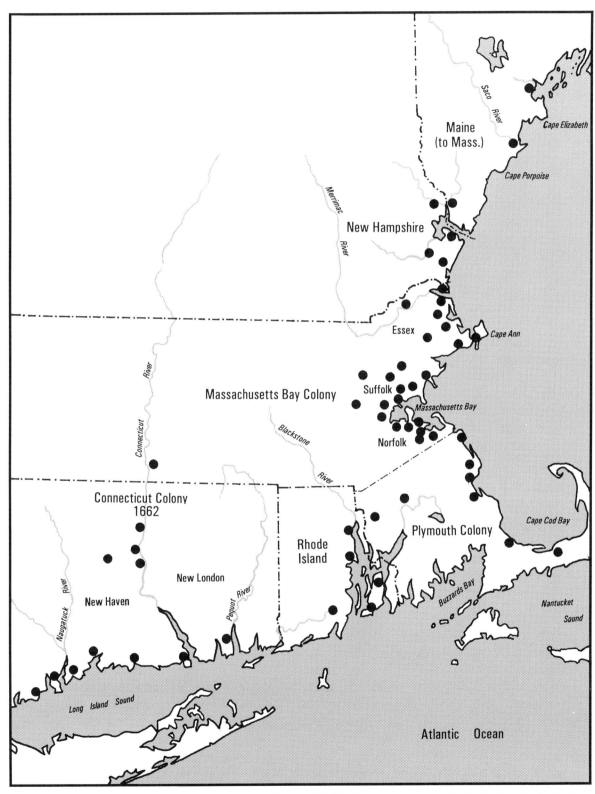

New England Settlements, 1620-1648. Americans with Yankee ancestors will find that their Puritan immigrant probably came to New England within five years of 1635. The New England settlements of the Puritans are shown above, representing the first towns settled in New England up to 1648. Note that virtually all of the settlements are near ocean bays, inlets, or rivers.

Scotia, north to Canada, and west to the Pacific. Along the way they founded the cities of Buffalo, Cleveland, Chicago, St. Paul, Denver, Salt Lake City, San Francisco, and Seattle. Today, most families of Yankee descent trace their American beginnings to an English ancestor who came ashore in Massachusetts Bay within five years of the year 1635." [2]

The Puritans hoped to build what they called a "New Zion" in America. They were escaping from religious persecution in England. Freedom to practice their religion was the main purpose for their coming to America. They truly felt they were building a "Bible Commonwealth" which might serve as a model for mankind. John Winthrop, who became governor of Massachusetts, left an exhortation which was to be memorized by many generations of New England schoolchildren: "We shall be as a City upon a Hill, the eyes of all people are upon us... we shall be a story and a byword throughout the world." [3]

The religous doctrine held by the Puritans was harsh and rigorous and was the civil code for the colony. But the Puritans still considered themselves part of the Church of England. They hoped to "purify" the church, hence their name. The basis of their Calvinist beliefs was that man was depraved, corrupted by Adam's original sin. They also believed in the Calvinist doctrine of Election — which held that only a few are chosen by God to be admitted to the Covenant, the contract with God offering salvation through Grace and Love. They believed the world was evil and that one must strive to live virtuously in a world of darkness. Puritans were expected to report the sins of their neighbors in church meetings to cleanse the community. In such a society, anyone not adhering to the harsh rules of conduct could be suspected of sinful deeds.

Most early immigrants to Massachusetts shared this highly personal sense of spirtual striving. Their puritism was even more rigourous than in the Calvinist churches of

Europe. A majority of the adults in most Massachusetts towns were able to meet the rigorous requirements for church membership. By 1648 in most of the towns, church members were at least 80 percent of all male taxpayers.

Massachusetts did more to screen the immigrants than other colonies in America. Those coming to this "City upon a Hill" were people who believed the right way. They thought of themselves as twice chosen people, once by God, once by the General Court of Massachusetts. Other English plantations eagerly welcomed any two-legged animal who could be dragged on board an emigrant ship. Massachusetts chose its colonists with care. In doubtful cases, the founders of the colony demanded written letters of recommendation.[4] Upon arrival in the colony, those who did not measure up were soon banished to other colonies or sent back to England.

The Puritan migrants were also unique in that they mostly paid their own passage to America. Unlike the thousands of servants coming to Virginia and Maryland, whose passage was paid by someone else, it is estimated that about 75 percent of the Puritan immigrants paid their own way. Again, this was not by accident. The founders of the Massachussetts Bay Colony did not want people immigrating who were unable to make their own way. This policy had other benefits: most of the adult males were literate, had a trade or profession, and could immediately begin a fruitful life in the colony.

The Origins of the Puritans

By examining the ship lists containing 2,885 immigrants to New England from 1629-1640, it can be determined that the Puritans came from nearly every county in England. Every county of England was represented except Westmoreland in the far north and Monmouth on the border of Wales. [5]

However, by closer examination, it can be learned that well over half of them came from one particular region. It lay on the east of England. The geographic center was the town of Haverhill, very near the point where three counties come together: Suffolk, Essex, and Cambridge. A circle drawn around the town of Haverhill with a radius of sixty miles will encircle the area where most New England immigrants lived. This area reaches east to Great Yarmouth on the coast of Norfolk County, north to Boston in eastern Lincolnshire County, west to Bedford County and Hertfordshire County, and south to the coast of East Kent. It is roughly the land described as East Anglia — Norfolk, Suffolk, Essex, Hertfordshire, Cambridgeshire, Huntingdonshire, and Lincolnshire, plus parts of Bedfordshire and Kent.

About sixty percent of the immigrants to Massachusetts came from these nine eastern counties, based on ship's lists and New England genealogies. The most concentrated region was the counties of Suffolk, Essex, and Norfolk, which accounted for nearly half of all immigrants. Also important was the part of East Lincolnshire which lay near the English town of Boston, and a triangle of Kent bounded by the towns of Dover, Sandwich, and Canterbury. These areas were the core of the Puritan migration to New England.[6]

Another group of Puritans came from a center of migration in the west country of England, very near where the counties of Dorset, Somerset, and Wiltshire come together. It is interesting that the Puritans who came from the west country of England mostly did not stay in the Massachusetts Bay area. They tended to move to Connecticut, or south to Nantucket, or north to Maine. The Puritans from the west country were not accustomed to the same cultures of the East Anglian immigrants nor were they as strict in their Puritan beliefs.

By playing with the percentages, one can generally conclude that the children and grandchildren of those Puritans who re-mained in the heart of Massachusetts were most likely children of migrants who came from East Anglia in England. Those who moved into other areas of New England soon after their arrival were originally from the west country of England.

The East Anglian origins for the settlers of Massachusetts before 1660 can be confirmed by the names they gave to their New England towns. Studies show that sixty percent of the town names before 1660 were borrowed names from East Anglia.[7] (The same percentage found for the origins of the immigrants taken from ship's lists and genealogies.) Examples of New England towns named after their counterparts in England are Ipswich, Groton, Boxford, Sudbury, Hadley, Wrentham, and Framingham from towns of the same names in Suffolk County, England. Town names taken from Norfolk, England, were Lynn, Newton, and Hingham. Other towns from East Anglia were Cambridge (Cambridge;) Dedham, Springfield, Topsfield, Braintree, Billerica, Chelmsford, and Malden (Essex).

Since the origins of the Puritan immigrants were limited to a handful of counties, searching for genealogical references in the surviving parish records of the East Anglian counties of England would be the logical place to start. If you have a New England ancestor who came to America within five years of 1635, your chances of locating a reference to him in English records will be greater in the parishes found in the counties of Norfolk, Suffolk, and Essex. After those three counties, one should then search the parish records of Hertfordshire, Cambridgeshire, Huntingdonshire, Lincolnshire, Bedfordshire, and Kent counties. Next in priority should be the parishes within the city of London. The next group to search, particularly for those immigrants who did not stay long in Massachusetts, would be the west country counties of Dorset, Somerset, and Wiltshire. Many parish records from these English counties have been microfilmed and are available for research through the

County Origins of the Puritans. About half of the English emigrants to New England during the Great Migration came from three East Anglian counties: Norfolk, Suffolk, and Essex. The center of migration was the town of Haverhill in Suffolk County. A circle with a sixty-mile radius with Haverhill as the center point defines the area where about 65-70 percent of the Puritans lived prior to their migration to America. This circle includes the suburbs and city of London. A secondary center of migration was an area where Somerset, Wiltshire, and Dorsett counties come together, in the west country of England.

Family History Library of Salt Lake City. To confirm what records exist, one should use the Family Search System electronic card catalog available at a Family History Center.

Transplanted Cultures

East Anglia was a region of England with some specific folkways, such as the methods of land division into towns, with strips of planting fields held by freemen and communal grazing fields (commons) for each village. This practice was followed in New England but not in Virginia. It was not an invention of New England. It was a cultural attribute carried to New England from the East Anglian counties in England.

Other cultures of East Anglia were continued in New England, such as foods: usually boiled or baked beans; clothing: generally simple dark colored attire; architecture: the "salt box" house; and many other ways of living. It is possible to visit parts of East Anglia today and see many of the same types of buildings that one can find in New England.

Even the manner of speech called the "Yankee Twang" came from East Anglia. When a New Englander talks about *Cuber* for *Cuba,* he is repeating a speech dialect inherited from East Anglia, England, from the 1500s. Other common pronounciations found in both East Anglia and New England are: *har* for *hair, ar* for *air, and war* rhymes with *star, ginral* for *general, yistidy* for *yesterday, darter* for *daughter, Americur* for *America.* These are all Yankee Twang pronounciations which are still common in New England today.

The Puritan practice of naming their children was also a carryover from East Anglia. The choice for names was usually from the Bible. The first son and daughter were named after their parents by at least two thirds of the settlers, a practice continued for many generations. If a child died, it was common for a later child to be named after the one who died. It was possible for New England parents to have had three sons named John, for example. These naming practices were not unique to New England but were repeated from naming practices already in place in the East Anglian part of England many years before the Puritans came to America.

The Puritans had an elite class who doubled as the spiritual and civil leaders of the society. But the elite was less important in comparison with Virginia society, where the elite ruled a working class of servants. In Massachusetts, a Puritan minister could not hold a political office, but in every other way their power was great. When a stranger asked Reverend Phillips of Andover if he was the parson who served the community, he replied, "I am, sir, the parson who rules here." [8]

Democracy existed in New England towns. Voting was conducted at town meetings by freemen, those men holding title to land. In general, land holdings were smaller than in other American colonies and with less differences between the wealthy and the poor. The size of farmland owned by freeman ranged from about 50 to 650 acres, with little distinction between the status of land holders in affairs of the community. The practice of town meetings, and a form of egalitarian community was not unique to New England. It was practiced first in the East Anglian region of England.

The Puritans disliked the English system of primogeniture, the practice of the eldest son inheriting the entire estate upon his father's death, particularly in intestate cases where there was no will. They preferred the method found in the book of Deuteronomy, which prescribed that a father should honor "the first born (son), by giving him a double portion of all that he hath." [9] It was rare for Puritans to include anyone outside of the immediate family in matters of inheritance. In colonial Virginia, one could find cousins, nieces, or nephews named in wills. In New England, the names given in a will were almost always the sons and daughters of the deceased only. Usually, sons received land, while the daughters received personal property, such as linen, china, or furniture. A woman could own land if named in a will; but if there were no will, a woman would rarely be granted land as part of an estate division. These differences were not invented in Massachusetts. They were transplanted from East Anglia where the Puritans had developed this particular manner of inheritance.

NOTES

1. John Winthrop, "General Observations for the Plantation of New England", *Winthrop Papers,* Vol. II, May 1629, page 114.

2. David Hackett Fischer, *Albion's Seed: Four British Folkways in America,* (Oxford University Press, 1989), page 17.

3. John Winthrop, "A Modell of Christian Charity Written on board the Arrabella on the Atlantick Ocean," *Winthrop Papers,* Vol. II, pages 282-95.

4. Some of these recommendations appear in Young, *Chronicles of the First Planters,* and in the *Winthrop Papers.*

5. Charles E. Banks, *Topographical Dictionary of 2885 English Emigrants to New England, 1620-1650,* (Philadelphia, 1937).

6. Ibid.

7. William H. Whetmore, "On the Origins of the Names of Towns in Massachusetts," *Massachusetts Historical Society Proceedings,* Vol. 12, pages 391-413.

8. Charles M. Andrews, *Pilgrims and Puritans,* (New Haven, 1926), page 166.

9. *Deuteronomy 21:16;* this was also their interpretation of *Genesis 48:22* where Israel said unto Joseph, the first born of the true wife, "I have given thee one portion of above thy brethern."

West Country Cavaliers

and their Servants to the

Chesapeake, 1641-1675

As the Puritan migration came to an end, another migration began. This time to Virginia. Late in 1641, Sir William Berkeley left London for Virginia to rule as governor, which he did for the next thirty-five years. During his tenure, the colony developed in a very different manner than the Puritan settlements. William Berkeley's station in life and his attitude about governing had a profound impact upon the development of Virginia.

Berkeley's manners were those of a courtier, polished by years in the presence of the King. His speech was that of a scholar, with Oxford learning; and he had the bearing of a soldier, knighted on the field of honor by Charles I. This proud cavalier was given the commission of Royal Governor of Virginia. He molded Virginia in the direction he wished, which was a duplication of the privileged way of life he knew in the west country of England. Berkeley was not the eldest son of his family; and therefore, he inherited nothing when his father died. Such "second sons" of England were destined to a life in the military or clergy. They were well-educated but without property. His brother, John Lord Berkeley, introduced him to the court, and the King was so impressed with him that he appointed him Gentleman of the Privy Chamber Extraor-

dinary. In 1639 he was knighted in the field at Berwick, and two years later became Royal Governor of Virginia. As a "second son," Berkeley fared very well indeed. Others of his station were not so fortunate, because the system of primogeniture left second sons without property or wealth in Somerset County, west of London, where Berkeley was born.

In February 1642 when Berkeley arrived in Jamestown, the colony of Virginia was a poor community of barely 8,000 people. The colony had gained a reputation "that none but those of the meanest quality and corruptest lives went there".[1] But Virginia was transformed. Berkeley played the leading role through his long years in office to build an ideal society which was an expression of his own values. He framed Virginia's political system, writing many of the laws himself. He also shaped the process of immigration to the colony during a critical period in its history. That process defined its culture and largely determined the Virginia way of life for generations to come.

Berkeley recruited a Royalist elite to Virginia, promising to the "second sons" of the west country of England a place to be rulers of a society that they could not accomplish in England. A cavalier migration continued

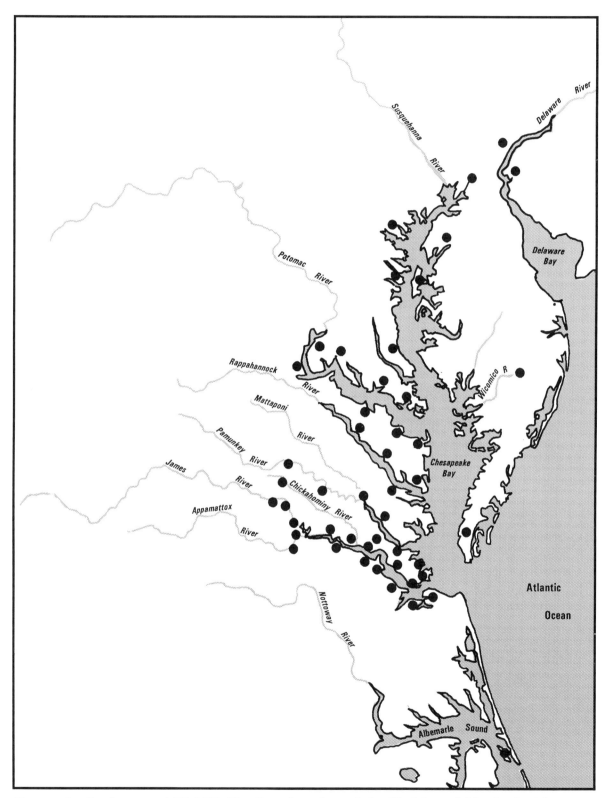

Chesapeake Settlements, 1607-1675. The first plantations of the Virginia and Maryland settlers were developed at the bottom lands near the rivers. The most desireable crop was tobacco, which was well suited to the fertile bottom lands.

through Berkeley's tenure as Governor, 1642-1676. Much of it occurred during the decade of the 1650s, when a Puritan leadership emerged from the Civil War in England and attempted to force their beliefs on the English people. The Royalists, like the Puritans had been during their "Eleven Years of Tyranny," now found themselves on the wrong political side in England. Some of these Royalists took refuge in Europe, but many were recruited by Sir William Berkeley of Virginia. Some had been his kinsmen and friends before they came to America. They shared his Royalist politics, his Anglican faith, and his vision for the future of the colony.

These "distressed cavaliers" founded what would later be called the First Families of Virginia, even though they were not the first colonists in Virginia. If most Yankee descendants can trace their beginnings to an immigrant to Massachusetts within five years of 1635, the beginning of most Virginia ruling families occured within ten years of the year 1655, when the important Chesapeake settlements began.

"The founder of the Carter family, for example, came over in 1649. His forebears had been rich in England; his children became still richer in Virginia. The first Culpeper also arrived in 1649; as did the first Hammond, Honywood, and Moryson. The first Digges migrated in 1650, together with the first Broadhurst, Chicheley, Custis, Page, Harrison, Isham, Skipwith, and Landon. The first Northampton Randolph appeared circa 1651, and the first Mason in 1652. The first Madison was granted land in 1653, the first Corbin in 1654. The first Washington crossed the ocean in 1657; he was John Washington, the younger son of an Oxford-trained clergyman who had been removed from his living by the Puritans. The family seat was Sulgrave Manor, a few miles north of Oxford. Also in 1657 arrived Colonel William Ball, the ancestor of George Washington's mother, and in 1659 the first Fairfax came.[2]

Every year of that troubled decade brought a fresh crop of cavaliers to Virginia. Of seventy-two families in Virginia's high elite whose dates of migration are known, two-thirds of them arrived between 1640 and 1669. A majority appeared between 1647 and 1660.

After the restoration of Charles II to the throne in 1660, Sir William Berkeley continued his recruiting campaign. In 1663 he published a pamphlet addressed to the younger sons of England's great families:

"A small sum of money will enable a younger brother to erect a flourishing family in a new world; and add more strength, wealth and honor to his native country, than thousands did before, that dyed forgotten and unrewarded in an unjust war... men of as good families as any subjects in England have resided there, as the Percys, the Barkleys, Chichelys, Moldsworths, Morrisons, Kemps, and hundreds of others which I forbear to name, lest I should misherald them in this catalogue."[3]

Sir William Berkeley's recruiting campaign was very successful. Nearly all of Virginia's ruling families were founded by younger sons of eminent English families during his governorship. The founders of Virginia were able to construct from Virginia the cultural system they were denied at home in England.

But you don't establish a ruling class in England or America without workers; and Berkeley's plan was to import workers to Virginia, without much regard for their station in life. Indentured servants were to be the primary work force for the elites who were bent on recreating an English Royalist society in America. Just as was done in the west country of England, the distressed cavaliers needed a large population of servants to plant, work, and harvest the fields and perform all other tasks that needed to be done. To encourage workers to come to the Virginia plantations, the ruling class offered grants of land to the servants — but not until the immigrant had completed a period of servitude to the one who had paid his passage to Virginia. In most cases, the servant was compelled to serve a period of seven years to the master. The land deeds recorded in the counties of Virginia and Maryland are full of references to the indentured servants coming from England to the plantations — an important genealogical source. What is not surprising is that the servants mostly came from the same area of England where the ruling families had lived.

The development of plantations in Maryland occurred simultaneously to those of Virginia; and the proprietory governor, Lord Baltimore, applied similar processes employed by William Berkeley. The exception in colonial Maryland was that it was founded by a Catholic, and Lord Baltimore allowed more religious tolerance than the other colonies of America. (That tolerance ended in 1692 when Catholics were purged from any political office and discouraged from immigration.) The plantations of Maryland progressed in the same manner as those of Virginia, and during the first few decades, the working class was primarily indentured servants rather than black slaves.

An indentured servant usually had a right to 50 acres of land which would be recorded in the county courthouse upon his arrival. The servant's right to land was incidental to the land owners, since the primary purpose of this system was an incentive to the land owners to increase the number of people immigrating to the colony as workers. Workers who were punished for misdeeds were often penalized with longer terms of servitude. The master received a number of acres "per head" for each person for whom he had paid passage to Virginia or Maryland. As a result, these land grants were called "headgrants."

Other court records during this era show that headgrants were often bought and sold.

A ship's captain might come to Annapolis or Jamestown with servants as an investment for profit. As the one providing for the servants' passage, he would be granted a certain number of acres of land per head, which he would then sell to planters soon after their arrival in Virginia or Maryland. Rights to land remained with the servant until he had completed his contract period of servitude. His contract could also be sold — and records exist for the early county records of Virginia and Maryland showing that servants were traded like slaves back and forth.

Black slavery came to Virginia and Maryland only after the importation of indentured servants could not keep up with the demand of the cavaliers to increase their holdings and as new lands were opened for planting. For example, in 1650 there were more slaves in Massachusetts than there were in either Virginia or Maryland. But by the late 1600s, the importation of African slaves had become the primary method of acquiring a work force for the plantations.

Unlike the village life being established in Massachusetts, the plantations of Virginia and Maryland were scattered, most of them at least 1,000 acres in size. A "great house" was the main feature of the plantation, surrounded by many out-buildings, and was a center for one basic family unit along with the servants' quarters. The preference for rural living was not something invented in Virginia or Maryland. It was transplanted from a particular area of England.

The Origins of the Virginia and Maryland Immigrants

The origins of Virginia and Maryland immigrants can be traced from virtually every county of England. But a majority of its ruling class and indentured servants came from only a few counties of England. A case in point was the population that settled in Virginia's Isle of Wight County. A local historian found that "the early Isle of

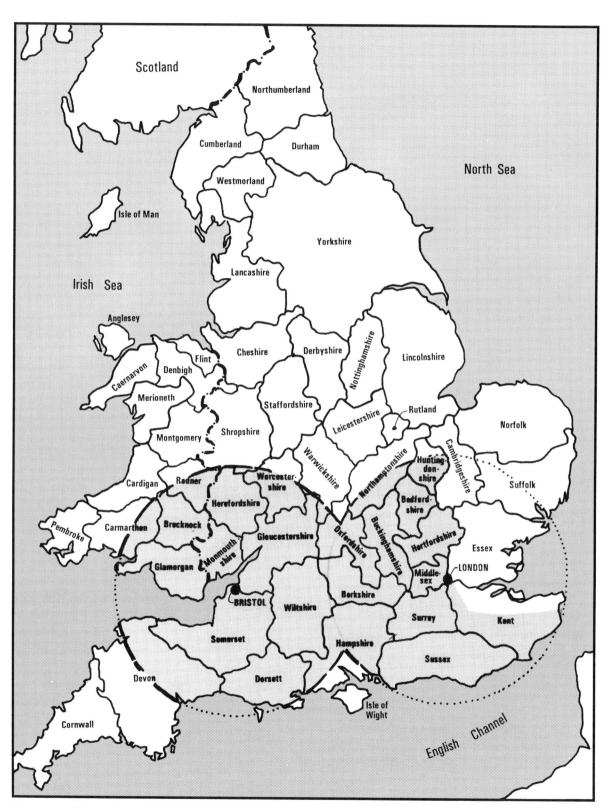

County Origins of the Virginia and Maryland Immigrants, 1641-1675. The Royalist/Cavalier society being formed in Virginia and Maryland was mainly a result of the English origins of the founders, where the same political and religious systems were in place. Before 1650, a majority of the emigrants, both masters and indentured servants, came from within a 60 mile radius of London, but excluding the East Anglia region. After 1650, the primary recruiting ground for servants was within a 60 mile radius of Bristol.

Wight families seems to have come mostly from the southwest of England, that is, the counties of Gloucester, Somerset, Devon, Dorset, Wiltshire, and Hampshire... their names appear to be more numerous in the west country than in any other part of England. After the west country, London and its surrounding counties seem to be next".[4]

Another example was the population of Berkeley Hundred in Virginia. Its historian found that "the majority... whether sponsors, tennants at labor or indentured servants, were... born and bred in Gloucester, where many of them were natives of the Berkeley Vale, the Cotswold Edge, or the Winchcombe area."[5]

These regional patterns changed a little during the mid-seventeenth century. One historian has suggested that before 1650 as many as 80 or 90 percent of Virginia's servants sailed from London; and the great majority came from the southwestern part of the country, particularly. London and the surrounding counties. Roughly half (52%) of those servants sailing from the River Thames identified their homes as London itself — mostly the suburbs. Only about 2 percent came from the inner city. The other half came mostly from counties to the west of London: Middlesex, Buckingham, Surrey, Berkshire, Oxfordshire, Warwickshire, and Northamptonshire. Hardly any Virginia or Maryland immigrants came from the Puritan stronghold of East Anglia.

After 1650 Bristol became more important in Virginia's servant trade. The great majority of emigrants from Bristol (87% in one sample) came from the west of England and south of Wales. The most important place of origin was the Severn Valley. The recruiting ground for Virginia's plantations could be defined by drawing two great circles around the cities of London and Bristol, each with a radius of roughly sixty miles. From the London circle, however, omit the Puritan domain of East Anglia, north of London.[6]

Transplanted Cultures

The ruling families of Virginia were mostly Royalists and adherents to the established Church of England. The parishes that were created to serve their religious communities followed the English system exactly, with a vestry appointed among church leaders to manage social and civil affairs. All landowners were taxed through their church parish to provide for the poor, the orphans, and the insane. In fact, the everyday lives of the first citizens of Virginia and Maryland were more under the scrutiny of the Anglican Church vestry than they were from the civil court system. The jurisdictional boundaries of Virginia counties and parishes were often the same. Therefore, genealogists will find that any surviving parish records are important sources. (The General Court of Virginia in Richmond, which was in the early years the same as Virginia's colonial legislature, was burned during the Civil War in 1865, and most of the civil records created during the early colonial period no longer exist. But since church records were maintained at the local level, many of the parish records have survived.)

The early Virginia and Maryland settlers had a different method of naming their children than was done in Massachusetts. Where the Puritans would rarely name a child after a king or any name not in the Bible, the Virginians followed a practice that had long existed in the west country of England. The same practices were followed by the ruling families and servants alike. Special favorites were the names of Teutonic warriors, Frankish Knights, and English Kings, such as William, Robert, Richard, Edward, George, and Charles — choices rarely made in Massachussets. The daughters of Virginians often received names of Christian saints who did not appear in the Bible and also traditional English folk names, such as Margaret, Jane, Catherine, Frances, and Alice — as well as the traditional favorites of Mary, Elizabeth,

Anne, and Sarah. This pattern of naming was not invented in Virginia or Maryland. It was the practice followed in the west country of England where the immigrants lived prior to coming to the Chesapeake.

One study of naming patterns in Middlesex County, Virginia finds that only 27 percent of eldest sons and 19 percent of first-born daughters were given the first names of their parents, compared with 67 percent in Massachusetts. But 60 percent of eldest sons in Virginia received their grandparents' names, compared with 37 percent in Massachusetts.[7] As a general rule, the first son was named after the father's father; the first daughter was named after the mother's mother. The second son was named after the father; the second daughter was named after the mother. By tracing families through several generations, a naming rhythm emerges in which every third generation repeats the same first names. Naming patterns observed in genealogies from the English counties where the Virginia immigrants came from are identical to those used in Virginia.[8]

It would be dangerous for genealogists to make assumptions since the naming practice was not followed 100 percent. However, when reoccurring first names appear in a pedigree in every third generation, it is an important clue to the common naming practices of colonial Virginia for that family line. Other closely related families, or other families living in the same area probably followed the same practice.

Early colonial Virginia and Maryland wills confirm the practice of primogeniture as the system of inheritance. An oldest son usually inherited his father's estate entirely. In the case of intestate files, where a man died without a will, the courts followed this practice nearly every time. However, a Virginia will could deviate from the practice of primogentiure and often did. Unlike the Puritans, Virginians were known for including bequests in their wills for people not necessarily part of their immediate family. Nieces, nephews, cousins, and even close friends may be mentioned in a colonial Virginia will (and unfortunately, not often telling the reader what their relationship was to the desceased). This practice was a carryover from the west country of England where the first Virginians originally lived.

NOTES

1. William Berkeley, *A Discourse and View of Virginia,* (London, 1663, reprinted 1914), page 3.

2. Dates of migration of 72 families in Virginia's high elite are found in Swem, *Virginia Historical Index,* Bruce, *Social Life in Virginia,* or Nell M. Nugent, *Cavaliers and Pioneers,* (Richmond, 1934).

3. Berkeley, *A Discourse and View of Virgina,* page 3.

4. Of families known to have settled in Isle of Wight County during the 17th century, 50% came from the five counties of Devon, Dorset, Gloucester, Somerset and Wilshire. Another 40% were from London and its environs. The rest of England contributed 10%. This data appears in John Bennett Boddie, *Seventeenth Century Isle of Wight County, Virginia,* (Baltimore: 1959), page 259.

NOTES, continued:

5. Eric Gethryn Jones, *George Thorpe and the Berkeley Company: A Gloucester Enterprise in Virginia,* (Gloucester, 1982).

6. David Hackett Fischer, *Albion's Seed: Four British Folkways in America,* (Oxford University Press, 1989), page 237.

7. Smith, *Child-Naming Practices,* page 550.

8. William Berry, *County Genealogies: Pedigrees of the Families in the County of Kent,* (London, 1830), pages 186-87.

North Midland Quakers to the Delaware Valley, 1675-1725

The third major migration to America, that of the English Quakers, began after the civil war in England and the restoration of King Charles II to the throne. The Society of Friends (Quakers) was founded by George Fox (1624-91), a Leicestershire weaver's son who developed his doctrine of the Inner Lights in 1646 and made his early converts mostly in the North Midlands of England. It is not surprising that a majority of the early Quakers who migrated to America also come from this part of England.

The residents of the North Midlands counties were a divided people. This area of England had a brutal history of division between the ruling elite and the governed dating from the time of the Norman conquest. The Normans had been preceeded as invaders by the Vikings and Norse traditions were still strong in this area of England in the 17th century. The North Midland rulers, however, remained Catholic, in rememberance of their French/Norman past; but the main population was fiercely independent and Protestant. North Midlanders strongly objected to the system of landlords, servants, and large manors brought to England by the Normans. This system had taken root in the southern areas of England and was particularly strong in the area from which the Virginia and Maryland plantation owners had lived in the west country of England.

In the North Midlands, however, private ownership of parcels of land for farming was wide-spread. As a result, a more egalitarian society existed there. In many ways, the North Midland region was similar to the East Anglia region in the practice of private land ownership. And, the North Midlanders practiced a form of democracy that was inherited from the Norse invaders centuries before the Normans — where the freemen gathered together in an open field and voted on some issue.

While the rest of England consisted mostly of Anglicans and Puritans, the North Midland area saw the rise of a diversity of new religious sects. Among the first of the sects were the Anabaptists, of whom many became Muggletonians, then Familists, Fifth Monarchy Men, Ranters, Seekers, and Quakers.

The establishment and evolution of these reactionary sects were a result of the rule of the Puritans from 1649 to 1660. Except for the Quakers, none of these sects were to survive long. After 1660 and the restoration of Charles II to the throne, religious tolerance was to become the law of the land. To some degree, religious tolerance did occur.

But, the large numbers of Quakers in the North Midlands still found themselves apart, mainly because of their aversion to paying tithes to support a different church than their own. Although the established churches acted as tax collectors for all farmers in a particular parish, the Quakers built and attended their own meeting houses and felt justified in ignoring the established churches. For this reason, many Quakers were persecuted and jailed for non-payment of taxes. During the 1660s and 1670s, Quaker lands in tax default were confiscated and sold, often for much more than the tax the land owner owed.

In virtually all other ways, the Quakers believed in peaceful coexistence with all other people and religions. But their lives were not complete in England. Historians argue as to the real reasons for the great migration of Quakers to America because most of the persecutions of the Quakers by the established churches had ended by 1675. Most agree, however, that the Quakers wanted to prove that their way of life could be accomplished better in a new environment without any hamperings from established rules of order.

Quaker belief was that of a personal experience with God, that man must be "born again" to have salvation. They believed that man would be guided by an "Inner Light." Unlike the Puritans, who believed that only the Elect could have salvation, and that not everyone could be qualified. The Quakers believed that anyone could receive salvation. For that reason and from their very beginnings, the Quakers sent missionaries and evangelists to all parts of Europe and America.

Quakers had been arriving in America as early as 1650. They were mostly wandering evangelists and missionaries who were punished cruelly in Puritan and Anglican communities just as they had been at home. There are recorded accounts of Quakers being put to death in Massachusetts in the 1650s, for the crime of being a Quaker.

William Penn

The most famous convert to Quakerism was William Penn, the founder of Pennsylvania. Penn was born in 1644 near the Tower of London, a place in which he would later be imprisoned for his faith. He was born into a violent world and very nearly made violence his career as a military officer. He distinquished himself in wars and revolutions in which his wealthy family was involved. His father was a naval officer who had served King Charles I as well as Cromwell and was rewarded with large estates in Ireland where William Penn was raised. By his birth and breeding, Penn was very much an English gentleman. He was trained as a swordsman and, in 1666, engaged in combat at the English mutiny at Carrickfergus where he so distinguished himself that he was recommended for a military post.

As a young man, Penn was raised to be a "Christian and a Gentleman" and his father sent him to Christ Church, Oxford to broaden his faith. Penn was expelled as a nonconformist when he refused to wear the required black robes and to attend cumpulsary chapel. Back in Ireland, Penn heard the Quaker preacher Thomas Loe and was converted to that faith. His father first tried "whipping, beating, and turning out of doors" to change his mind. Penn did not waver and quickly became a leader among Friends. He preached throughout England and published more than 100 works.

He was often jailed by the authorities. In 1668 he was locked in the Tower of London for writing a Quaker book. He spent the time writing another one, *No Cross, No Crown,* which is known as his greatest work. Soon after his release in 1670, he was arrested again for preaching outside a locked meetinghouse in London. In the trial that followed Penn conducted his defense so brilliantly that jurors refused to convict him even with the threat of prison to themselves. The case became a landmark in the history of trial by jury.

Arrested again in 1671, he was secretly tried and sentenced to Newgate where he refused the privileges of his rank and lived in a common cell. There he finished *The Great Case of Liberty and Conscience,* one of the most noble arguments for religious liberty ever written. While suffering for his faith, Penn was treated with deference by his persecutors and affection by his jailors. He maintained a friendship with King Charles II and the future James II. While still in jail, he courted and married Gulielma Springett, a high-born lady who shared his Quaker faith. Her many connections gave him much influence in English society and helped him to secure the charter of Pennsylvania. After her death, Penn married Hannah Callowhill, a rich Bristol heiress who brought him an annual income sufficient to keep his colony afloat.

In 1671 Penn traveled to Europe and met with German Pietists who also suffered greatly from persecution. In company with them, he began to think seriously about founding a colony in America. He became a trustee in the West Jersey colony and drew up the fundemental laws of that colony. By 1675 William Penn was already involved with transplanting Quakers to North America and had purchased parcels of land in West Jersey. He petitioned his friend, King Charles II, for a charter for a formal colony in America. It was granted in 1681. The King, in his own hand, added the prefix "Penn" to the "Sylvania" which Penn had proposed as the name of his colony.

William Penn played the leading role in the development of Pennsylvania. He functioned as lawgiver, social planner, organizer, tireless promoter, and regulator of the immigration process. Like Sir William Berkeley had done for Virigina, Penn set the mode of migration and the social order of the colony, which continued even after the Quakers had become a minority group in Pennsylvania. Compared to other English colonies in America, the difference in Pennsylvania was that the process of building the colony was based on a Quaker way of life under the guidance and charismatic leadership of William Penn.

Quaker Folkways

The Quakers came to America with some specific folkways and traditions. An image comes to mind of the Quaker Oats gentleman dressed in black with a wide-brim hat, and speaking with "thee" and "thou", a stereotype we might consider unique to Pennsylvania Quakers. Not so, because these attributes were carried to America by immigrants from a specific area of England.

In the North Midlands of England, the farmers had a reputation for independence and a custom of equality among themselves. The family and farmhands all ate together at simple meals of boiled porridge and oakcakes. They dressed alike, in simple homespun suits and dresses of a distinctive color called "hodden gray." Their houses were sparsely furnished, and their culture made a virtue of simplicity and plain speech. All of these folkways became a part of Quakerism.

For example, the manner of speech in 17th century England was highly regionalized into several distinctive areas. Even today, there are still words used in these areas of England that are unique to each region. By the middle 1600s, Shakespearian English and the language of the King James version of the Bible had undergone changes, particularly in the southern parts of England. An example is the formal and familiar forms of *to you, you are,* or *you have.* The familiar forms were *to thou, thou art,* or *thou hast* which were used only to a family member or close friend. In 1675 these familiar forms of speech had not been dropped in the North Midlands of England and were still used in everyday speech. In contrast, The Puritans of East Anglia had dropped these forms long before their Great Migration to America. When the Quakers came to America, they brought the same manner of speech that was used in the North Midlands of England. So, the "thee" and "thou" of Pennsylvania Quakers was really the normal way of speaking to an immigrant from the North Midlands of England.

Origins of the English Quakers

The first large contingents of Quakers to migrate to America came to what is now New Jersey, on the east side of the Delaware River. It began with the first ship-load in 1675, which had sailed from London. The first settlement was named Salem (from the Hebrew Shalom). By 1681 some 1,500 Quakers had arrived in West Jersey. They were not the first to establish colonies there, however. As early as 1625, there had been colonies established by the Swedes and Dutch in what became East Jersey. But in West Jersey, the establishment of settlements was to become predominately Quakers. It is estimated that the annual Quaker migration between 1675 and 1700 was about the same as the Puritans' Great Migration to New England, about 20 shiploads per year, each with about 100 passengers.

Although the Friends' Migration is best known for the establishment of settlements in West Jersey and Pennsylvania, many Quakers migrated directly to the tideland areas of Virginia and North Carolina. For example, Nansemond County, Virginia, and Perquimans and Pasquotank counties of North Carolina were mostly inhabited by Quakers before 1700. Quakers became an important part of North Carolina's population up to 1800 when most of them left because of their opposition to slavery. As a result, Quakers were to become early settlers of the new free states, such as Ohio and Indiana, created from the old Northwest Territory.

The Quaker founders of Pennsylvania and New Jersey came from every part of England, but one English region stood out from the rest. The Friends' migration drew heavily from the North Midlands and especially from the contiguous counties of Cheshire, Lancashire, Yorkshire, Derbyshire, and Nottinghamshire. In one list of English immigrants who arrived in Philadelphia between the years 1682 and 1687, more than 80 percent came from these five counties. Only a few came from the south and west of England, and none were from East Anglia.

The same pattern appeared among immigrants who settled in Bucks County before 1687. Two-thirds came from the counties of Yorkshire, Lancashire, Cheshire, Derbyshire, Nottinghamshire, and Staffordshire. The rest were mainly from the area of London and Bristol. None were from the Puritan stronghold of East Anglia, the area of England that had supplied most of the immigrants to Massachusetts.

Other lists such as meeting certificates, ministerial rosters, servants' registers, and shipping lists, confirm the origins as the North Midlands. Of Quaker missionaries who were recognized by the Philadelphia Yearly Meeting, over half came from five northern counties: Cumberland, Westmoreland, Durham, Lancashire, and Yorkshire. A sizeable number came from English settlements in Ireland near Dublin. But, only ten percent came from East Anglia; and barely five percent came from those counties of southwestern England which contributed so heavily to the settlement of Virginia and Maryland.

On the banks of the Delaware River, Quakers generally distributed themselves in settlements according to their origin in Britain. Country Quakers from Cheshire, Lancashire, and Yorkshire settled mainly in Chester and Bucks counties. The rich uplands in these two counties were a reminder of the dales of northern England. London Quakers preferred the city and county of Philadelphia. Emigrants from Bristol founded a town of the same name on the Delaware River. Dublin Quakers occupied Newton, New Jersey. Quaker emmigrants from Wales colonized the "Welsh Tract,"

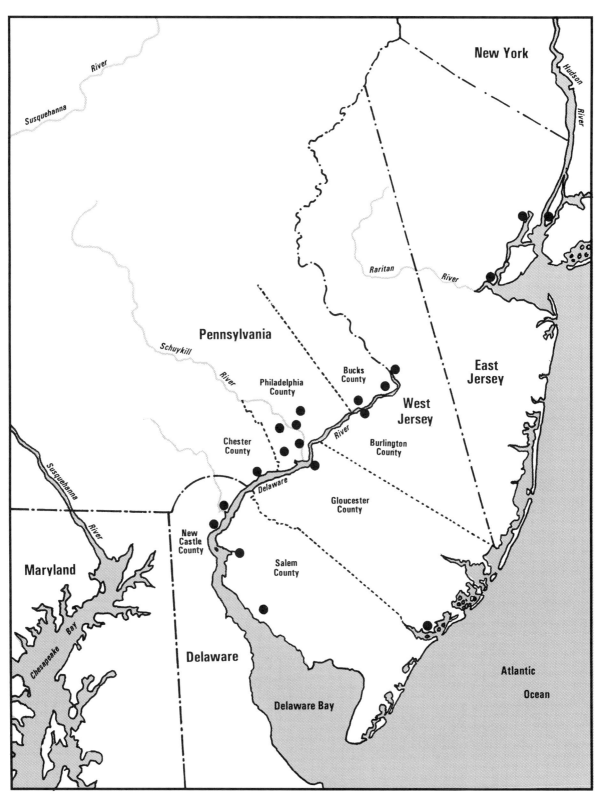

Quaker Settlements in America, 1675-1715. William Penn's first organized settlements in America were concentrated on both sides of the Delaware River. These colonies were settled primarily by immigrants from England, but with several boatloads of Rhineland Germans as well.

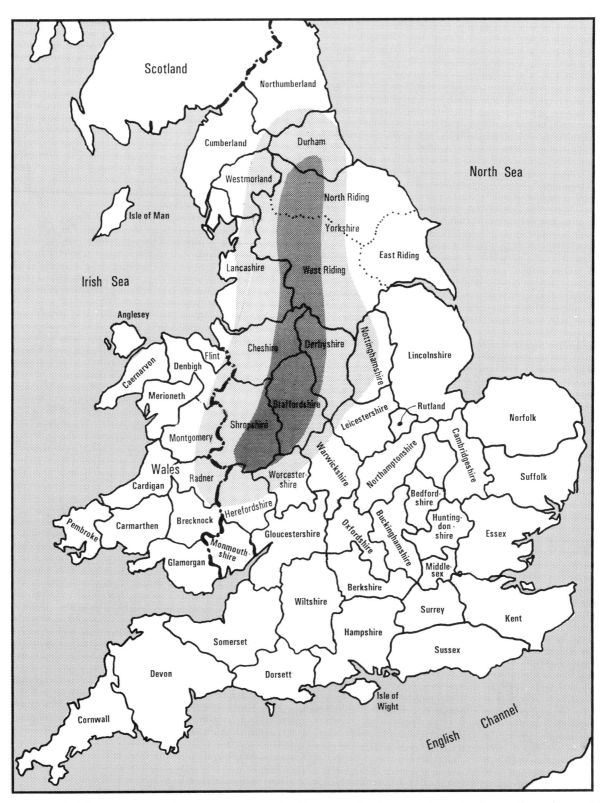

County Origins of the Quakers, 1675-1725. The North Midlands area of England was the origins of most of the Quaker emigrants to William Penn's settlements in America. The Pennine Range, represented by the inner, darker shaded area, supplied the largest group of Quakers during this period.

west of the Schuykill River.

The origins of these immigrants may also be observed in some of the names that they gave to their counties. Some examples are Chester, York, and Lancaster in Pennsylvania; Burlington, Cumberland, and Monmouth in New Jersey; and Newcastle in Delaware. In contrast, the northeastern New Jersey region settled mainly by New England Puritans was in Essex County, reflecting their East Anglian background. New Castle County, Delaware, reflects its Quaker beginnings, while Delaware's two other counties in the south, Kent and Sussex, were begun by the same type of settlers who were immigrating to Virginia and Maryland and who had their origins in the west country of England.

But also in contrast, Bergen and Somerset counties, in northern New Jersey, were first settled by the Dutch West Indies Company. Both counties were inhabited by Dutch-speaking communities. As much as 75 percent of the population spoke Dutch well into the 1700s, as did several communities along the Hudson River in New York.

Town or township names also reveal the North Midlands origins of the Quaker communities established in Pennsylvania and West Jersey. For example, Alston, Billton, Birmingham, Bradford, Bristol, Burlington, Carlisle, Chester, Chesterfield, Darby, Durham, Edgemont, Kennet, Leeds, Liverpool, Marple, Morland, Newcastle, Ridley, Sheffield, Trenton, and York were named after similar places in the North Midland counties of England.

The Quakers from Wales tended to flock together in what was called the Cambry or Welsh Tract. The earliest village names of this district defined the region of origin in the mother country: Flint, Montgomery, Bala, Tredyffrin, Radnor, Haverford, and Denbigh. Most of these names can be traced to northern and eastern Wales, just across the River Dee from Cheshire in England.

The most important area of the North Midlands that contributed the majority of the Quakers to America was the Pennine uplands which ran in a northerly direction from the Peak District of Derbyshire to the Fells of Yorkshire and Cumbria. This was the highest ground in England. It encompassed the six counties of Derbyshire, Nottinghamshire, Lancashire, East Cheshire, West Yorkshire, and southern Westmoreland. (The Pennines were the setting for the book *Wuthering Heights,* and *Jane Eyre* was set in the West Riding of Yorkshire.) Later, in the modern era, this area became the industrial heartland of Britain. Today it is an urban sprawl encompassing cities such as Manchester, Bradford, Sheffield, and Leeds, each with rows and rows of brick tenements stretching over the rolling hills. In the 17th century, however, this was one of the poorest rural areas of England, where small farmers struggled to feed themselves and produce a small surplus of wool for the market.

The Friendly Germans

Another early group of immigrants to Pennsylvania were the Rhineland Germans recruited by William Penn. They went by several different names, including *German Pietists, Palatines,* or the *Pennsylvania Dutch.* They came from the region of Germany bordered by Holland, the lowlands of Germany called the Palatinate (today, the Pfaltz-Rhineland region). They spoke a version of Low German, which was closer to Flemish or Dutch (or English) than the High German spoken in the modern Germany of today. In religious practice, they were comparable with the French Protestants called Huguenots. Many of the Germans were Quaker converts from William Penn's evangelism in German in the 1670s. Others who came were not Quakers, but they had a great attraction to the Quakers and shared many of their beliefs. The Friends called them "Friendly" Germans. In fact, the early Palatine immigrants often attended Quaker meetings rather than build their own churches.

The community of Germantown was the first settlement by German Quakers in Pennsylvania, which was founded in 1683. They also founded the towns of Cresheim, Crefeld, and Sommerhausen, named after the communities very near the present German - Dutch border which had expelled them.

After 1715 more Germans and other non-Quaker colonists began to arrive in Pennsylvania in growing numbers. Among them were British and Scottish Borderers who have been called Scotch-Irish. The Quakers heartily disliked these people and hurried them on their western way. (The next chapter will give more details about what happen to them.) Other ethnic groups entered Pennsylvania at a rapid rate and also left their names on the land. A few Swedish names survived, such as Christiana. In the mid-18th century, the Scotch-Irish would leave their names on the landscape. But the North Midland origins of the Quaker colonists may still be seen in the place names of the Delaware Valley, even to our own time.

The Quakers dominated the Delaware Valley for some 70 years, but by 1745 they had become a minority. In 1750 Philadelphia had a population of over 30,000 people and was the largest city in the British Empire except London. As a port, Philadelphia became the direct link to the interior of America for people of all nationalities coming to America. But, the Pennsylvania way of living was established by the Quakers who founded the first communities on the Delaware River and was to continue for decades thereafter.

Quaker naming patterns: Quakers named their children in a way much different than did the Puritans. While at least two-thirds of the early Puritans named a first born son after his father, and the first daughter after her mother, the Quakers followed a system similar to the Virginia and Maryland plantation settlers, with some variation. A first-born Quaker son, in the majority of cases, was named after his grandfather; but there was no rule as to whether the paternal or maternal side of the family went first. A first son could be named after the father's father or the mother's father. A first daughter was named after one of her grandmothers in the same manner.

Quaker inheritance patterns: In the first laws of East Jersey and Pennsylvania, the practice was of double partible inheritance, widow's thirds, and small shares for children other than the oldest son. This was much the same practice as was followed in the New England colonies. It differed from the practice of primogeniture followed in Virginia and Maryland, where the oldest son generally inherited his father's entire estate. "Double Partible" inheritance is the giving of a double share to the oldest son. In all of the English colonies, the "widow's third" was practiced, based on the English common law followed for centuries throughout Britain. A widow was entitled to one-third of her deceased husband's estate. In later laws, by the 1730s, the older system gave way to a more egalitarian system of equal shares for each child of a desceased's estate, which was more in keeping with the Quaker way of doing things. Quaker daughters were rarely given land in a will.

Quaker Marriages

The Quakers brought to America a strict set of marriage customs. Because of their distrust of English civil laws and their separation from the established Church of England, the first Quakers developed a process for marriages that was entirely within the framework of the Quaker meetings. George Fox wrote no fewer than sixty epistles about marriage. William Penn and other leaders frequently addressed the themes of who, when, where, and how to marry.

Quaker meetings were held often, as many as three times per week. They were conducted not only for worship but for the business of the community. Worship meetings were attended by both men and women, although seated separately. Business sessions were separated into men's and women's meetings. Written logs to these business meetings were recorded. Log entries were kept for subjects and the names of people involved in discussions or to record a decision that had been made. Genealogists will find a wealth of information about the Quakers because a large number of the recorded logs have survived. (Many of the various Quaker meeting logs were abstracted in Wade Hinshaw, *Encylcopedia of American Quaker Genealogy.* Hinshaw's volumes, now published by Genealogical Publishing Co., Inc., of Baltimore, exist for Pennsylvania and several other states.) Recorded Quaker meeting logs, which include marriage notices, represent the most important set of records for determining relationships.

The rule against outmarriage was strictly enforced by Quakers in America. For nearly two centuries, half of all of the disciplinary proceedings among Pennsylvania Quakers were about problems of courtship and marriage with "unbelievers". The rule against outmarriage was grounded not so much as a way of excluding other people, but in the Quaker belief that marriages should be founded in true Christian love, which they thought could only be accomplished between believers.

A proper Quaker marriage had no fewer than sixteen stages. When a man and woman agreed to marry, their first formal step was to consult their parents. If all agreed, the couple announced their intention to marry before the women's meeting. After an interval which gave the community time to digest the news, a female Friend formally sent a notice to the men's meeting. The couple then presented themselves before the men's meeting and announced their intention to marry. Thereafter, the men's meeting consulted the parents of both partners. Un-

less approval was given in writing, a marriage could not proceed. If either partner came from another meeting, the men's meeting also solicited "certificates of cleanliness" from that body. This process required a second session of the men's meeting, so that overseers could report on their inquiries. At this stage, a waiting period began during which others were given time to make objections. Then the men's meeting formally considered the question and agreed either to approve or forbid the union. This was called "passing the meeting," and was a great event. The wedding could now proceed. The recorded logs of the various Quaker meetings indicated the various steps that couples were going through. Their names and the names of their parents were mentioned in the process.

Stages of Quaker Beliefs

The Quaker way changed over the years. Historians of Quakerism identify four stages the religious order went through. The first was the founding of the sect (ca 1646-66) when Quakerism tended to be radical, evangelical, and messianic. The second stage (ca 1666-1750) was the flowering period, when the Society of Friends became increasingly institutional, rational, progressive, optimistic, enlightened, liberal, and actively involved in the world without losing its godly purposes. The third stage (ca 1750-1827) was an era when Quakers turned inward upon themselves and grew increasingly sectarian, exclusive, and perfectionist. A fourth stage of denominational division followed the Hicksite separation of 1827.

Of these four stages, the most important for American history was the second (ca 1666-1750), when the cultural institutions of the Delaware Valley were created. During this period, many Quakers kept slaves and there was no formal Quaker policy against bearing arms. It was the third period of Quakerism (ca 1750-1827), in which the Quakers became pacifists and opposed slavery as a matter of religious conviction. During the American Revolution, Quakers who refused to sign an Oath of Allegiance to the American cause (which included a promise to bear arms against its enemies if called upon) were branded as "Loyalists," even though most Quakers really did not fall into this category at all. As a result, some Quakers were persecuted and many fled America for sanctuary in Upper Canada (now Ontario) along with thousands of Loyalists from New England, New York, and Pennsylvania.

REFERENCES
Quakers to the Delaware Valley, 1675-1725

Braithwaite, William C., *The Beginnings of Quakerism,* (London, 1912).

Fischer, David Hackett, *Albion's Seed: Four British Folkways in America,* (Oxford, 1989).

Frost, J. William, *The Quaker Family in Colonial America,* (New York, 1973).

Gaustad, Edwin S., *Historical Atlas of Religion in America,* (New York, rev. ed., 1976).

Jones, Rufus, ed., *The Quakers in the American Colonies,* (New York, rpt, 1966).

Illick, Joseph E., *Colonial Pennsylvania,* (New York, 1976).

Penn, William, "A Further Account of the Province of Pennsylvania," in Albert Cook Myers, Ed., *Narratives of Early Pennsylvania, West New Jersey, and Delaware, 1630-1707,* (New York, rprt 1967).

Pomfret, John E., *The Province of West New Jersey, 1609-1702,* (Princeton, 1956).

Marietta, Jack D., *The Reformation of American Quakerism, 1748-1783* (Philadelphia, 1984).

Myers, Albert Cook, *Quaker Arrivals in Philadelphia, 1682-1750,* (Philadelphia, 1902).

Vann, Richard, "Quakerism: Made in America?," in Richard S. Dunn and Mary Maples Dunn, eds., *The World of William Penn,* (Philadelphia, 1986).

British and Scottish Borderers to America, 1717-1775

The fourth and largest group of immigrants from the British Isles were those who came to America's backwoods beginning about 1717 and continuing up to 1775. Some historians describe these immigrants as "Ulster Irish" or "Northern Irish." It is true that many sailed from the province of Ulster in northern Ireland, but these labels are not accurate when applied to the movement as a whole. More frequently, historians call these people "Scotch-Irish." That expression is an Americanism, rarely used in Britain, and still causes some ambiguity in describing the group as a whole.

From 1717-1775 historians estimate that at least 150,000 people came to America directly from the Ulster counties of northern Ireland, departing from the seaports of Belfast, Londonderry, Newry, Larne, or Portrush. But during this same period, another 75,000 people departed from ports along the coast of Scotland, such as Kirkcudbright and Wigtown. Meanwhile, another 50,000 came from northern English seaports such as Liverpool, Maryport, Morecambe, and Whitehaven.[1] What these groups had in common was that they all lived on or near the Irish Sea, and were all former residents of the borderlands of Scotland and England.

Of the entire migration from the Irish Sea of some 275,000 immigrants, less than half of them could rightfully be called "Scotch-Irish," the name most often given to the Ulster Irish immigrants. Even the "Irish" designation is inaccurate. These people did not think of themselves as Irish; and in fact, they were not. "We're no Eerish bot Scoatch," one of them was heard to say in Pennsylvania.[2] To further complicate the matter, a greater number of the Ulster Irish emigrants were originally from the border counties of northern England, not Scotland; and this group could be called "Anglo-Irish".

Perhaps a better description would be to call these people "borderers". It is a problem to give them a label at all. On the English side of the border, the people living there to this day will not call themselves "English". And it is probably true that their genealogy, traditions, and culture is more Scottish than English. For centuries, the borderlands passed back and forth between Scotland and England. Although English has been the language of the lowlands of Scotland and northern England, on both sides of the border the people have had more kinship with Scotland than England. Because of this, a description of the British and Scottish borderers who went to northern Ireland as "Scotch-Irish" may not be accurate, but it still describes the borderers without too much difficulty. Virtually all of them saw themselves as Scots.

The clan people from the lowland Scottish borders, the northern British borderers, and those transplanted to northern Ireland were so alike in their speech, religion, clothing, and demeanor that they could not be distinquished from one another by the colonial Americans they joined, and were simply lumped together as "Scotch-Irish."

A Brief History of the Borderers Move to Northern Ireland

The history behind the transfer of large groups of people from the borderlands of Scotland and England to northern Ireland dates back to the reign of King James I (1566-1625). He was James I of England but was also James VI of Scotland, son of Mary, Queen of Scots. He ascended to the throne in England after the death of his cousin, Queen Elizabeth I, in 1603. The era of James I was the first time that Scotland and England were ruled by the same monarch. It was also a time in which the Puritans of England began asserting themselves, although without much success until the demise of James' son, Charles I. Ironically, James I is known for the Bible that was translated and published during his reign, yet history has not given him much credit for being very "holy" — he was a monarch who delighted in declaring his "devine right" to rule in any way he saw fit. (His son, Charles I, followed his father's philosophy to the point of losing his head over it.)

It was also during the reign of James I that the British annexation of northern Ireland took place. By acquiring northern Ireland, King James saw himself as real estate agent. In the early 1600s he took advantage of the opportunity to enrich himself by selling a title to anyone with the money to buy one, and by granting large estates of land in northern Ireland. He then encouraged these newly titled English Dukes and Earls to import farm workers from the borderlands of Scotland and England. Workers were encouraged to move to Ireland by the promise of long-term leases to land. The estates established in northern Ireland allowed a tenant family to retain the right to farm a parcel of land and pass their tenancy from father to son for a period of 100 years.

King James I envisioned the plan to put English-Scottish borderers on English-controlled estates in northern Ireland. But he also saw northern Ireland as a perfect place to relocate thousands of troublesome borderers for another reason. The English-Scottish borderers had been a pain in the side of every Scottish and English monarch for centuries. The people there just did not seem to want to be "civilized" and were more interested in fighting wars, stealing cattle, or raiding their neighbors. If they could be encouraged to settle down in northern Ireland, perhaps the border between England and Scotland could be peaceful for the first time.

Very few migrations from the border region to northern Ireland continued after the reign of James I. In fact, it was not until the early 1700s, when England and Scotland officially became unified as one country, that large numbers of borderer clans were again transplanted to northern Ireland. The culture and traditions from the Scottish and English borderlands were carried across the Irish Sea to the northern Ireland counties of Antrim, Armagh, Derry, Donegal, Down, Fermanagh, and Tyrone. None of the transplants saw themselves as "Irish."

Origins of the Borderers

In 1915 an English folklorist named Cecil Sharp traveled to America's Appalachian highlands, collecting songs and dances of the back settlers of southwestern Pennsylvania, West Virginia, and the Carolinas. After careful comparision with British materials, he determined that their traditional songs, ballads, dances, singing-games, etc., came from the borderlands of Scotland and England. They were identical.[3]

The borderlands where these same traditions existed can be identified as a region of the far north in England, including most of the counties of Cumberland, Northumber-

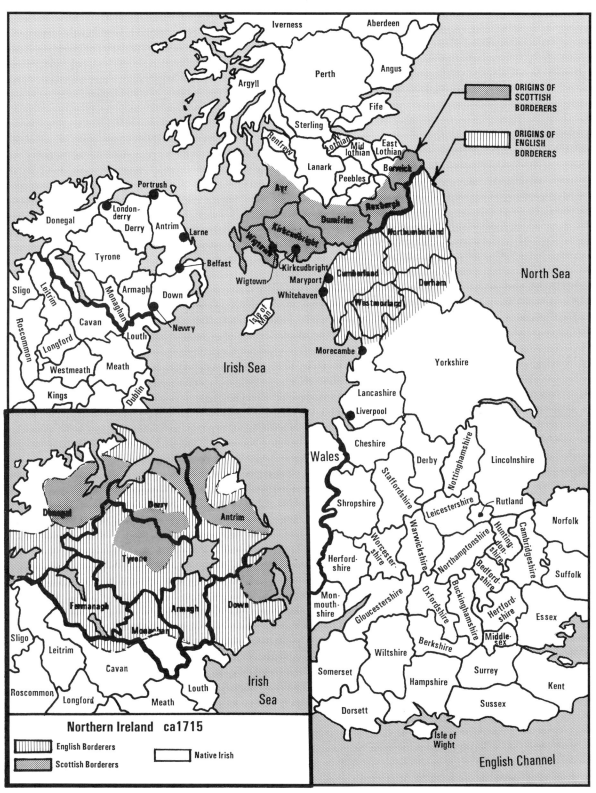

British-Scottish Borderlands and Northern Ireland. The original homes of the "Scotch-Irish" were on both sides of the border. These were the origins of the transplanted borderers to Northern Ireland, and the borderers who later migrated to America. The inset indicates the location of the native Irish, English Borderers, and Scottish Borderers in Northern Ireland just prior to their mass migration to America.

land, and Westmorland plus parts of Durham, Lancashire, and Yorkshire counties. It also included areas within six counties of lowland Scotland: Ayr, Berwick, Dumfries, Kirkcudbright, Roxburgh, and Wigtown.

These same counties of northern England and lowland Scotland were the original homes of thousands of people who had gone to live in northern Ireland prior to their migration to America. Yet, the traditions and cultures that Cecil Sharp identified in the backwoods areas of America were clearly from the border regions of England and Scotland, not Ireland. Therefore, it is clear that the migration of borderers to northern Ireland did nothing to change their border ways. They never adopted Irish customs nor thought of themselves as Irish. Even after a hundred years in Ireland, these transplanted "Scotch - Irish" followed their same border traditions and cultures.

Borderlands Culture

Before and after their migrations to northern Ireland, the nature of the people who originally inhabited the borderlands of England and Scotland was the same. "English and Scots borderers had everything in common except nationality," wrote historian George Fraser. "They belonged to the same, small, self-contained, unique world, lived by the same rules, and shared the same inheritance." [4]

Most of all, the borderlands of Scotland and England shared a common history of violence. For seven centuries, the kings of Scotland and England could not agree who owned it and meddled constantly in each other's affairs. From the year 1040 to 1745, every English monarch but three suffered a Scottish invasion or became an invader himself. For over 700 years, until after 1745, the region never had fifty consecutive years without war. (See box, next page.)

The battles between the monarchs of England and Scotland were only a part of the struggles in the borderlands. On both sides of the border, clan wars were frequent, especially in the "debatable lands" (an area between Dumfries County, Scotland, and Cumberland County, England) that was claimed by both kingdoms. In the debatable lands, powerful clans such as the Taylors, Bells, Grahams, and Bankheads lived outside the law, and were said to be "Scottish when they will, and English at their pleasure." [5] Other family clans specialized in the theft of livestock or as it became known on the border — "rustling."

Centuries of unending violence and lawlessness along the border shaped a social system which was different from that in other parts of the British Isles. The thanes, or heads of the clans, acted as warlords and controlled the countryside. These landlords owned the land. Small farming plots were held by the tenants, who were both farmers and warriors. Rents were paid by the farmers to the landlord usually in the form of a share of the crop produced. Tenancy of land parcels held by the borderers was passed from generation to generation because the inheritance system was double-partible, in which the eldest son in a family received a double share of the land, while younger sons received shares as well. This tended to maintain a constancy in land tenants as well as a continuing source of worker-warriors for the clan warlords.

The ancient family clans along the Scottish border were the Armstrongs, Beatties, Bells, Burns, Carlisles, Davisons, Dixons, Elliotts, Grahams, Hendersons, Humes, Johnstones, Kerrs, Littles, Maxwells, Olivers, Pringles, Robsons, Rutherfords, Scotts, Taits, Trotters, and Youngs.

On the English side, the main clans were the Armstrongs, Bells, Charltons, Collingwoods, Dacres, Dodds, Dunnes, Fenwicks, Forsters, Grahams, Grays, Herons, Hetheringtons, Milburns, Nixons, Nobles, Ogles, Potts, Ridleys, Robsons, Selbys, and Tailors.

To live in a country with such a long history of violence, the natives of such a land had to be ready to fight a battle at a moment's notice. The battle could be with a rival clan, invading armies, or some group seeking to get even for a previous wrong. "Blood battles" replaced legal institutions. The borderers settled their disputes with feud violence and blood money. There was a system which the borderers called "blackmail," involving the payment of protection money to powerful clans. As a result, family relationships became a matter of life and death. The only people who could be trusted had to be relatives, or members of the clan. Over a period of centuries, the borderlands produced people who learned to live with wars and violence. They became a distinctively hardened and resilent people. In addition to their battles, they developed some unique and interesting ways of living. Their borderland characteristics did not change much when they came to America.

The gentry of the borderlands were almost the only families with permanent dwellings. They built stone towers, called "peles," three to four stories high. The ground floor was a windowless storeroom with walls ten feet thick. Stacked above it was a hall for living, a bower for sleeping, and a deck for fighting. A few of them still stand today.

Most families living in the borderlands built their houses in a day or two, by erecting crude log or dirt structures

700 years of violence in the borderlands

☛ Scotland's first king, Duncan (1034-40), was murdered by Macbeth after losing a war to the Northumbrians.

☛ In 1057 Macbeth was killed after his defeat at Dunsinae.

☛ Scottish King Malcolm Canmore invaded England five times in hopes of conquering its northern provinces but was slain in Northumberland in 1093.

☛ By 1097, the Normans invaded the borderlands, and when Scotland's king Donald Bane resisted, they took him captive and put out his eyes to quiet him.

☛ In 1136, after an interval of peace, Scotland's King David led an army into England and fighting began again. During the next century most towns on both sides of the border were brutally sacked and burned, and the countryside was ravaged.

☛ In 1215, England's King John marched north on a mission of revenge. The Scottish burghers of Berwick were put to death by torture and the English set fire to their houses.

☛ During the 13th century, Scotland was forced to accept English control which brought another interval of restless peace. Conditions improved during the reign of Alexander II, a golden age for Scottish culture. But in 1286, Alexander fell to his death and the slaughter began again.

☛ England's King Edward I (1272-1307) captured the border town of Berwick and put to death every male of military age. For three centuries Scottish soldiers fought with the cry, "Remember Berwick!"

☛ The borderlands remained in English hands until about 1297, when Scotland's national hero William Wallace invaded Cumberland. His soldiers flayed the bodies of English officers who fell into their hands. But when Wallace himself was captured, his body was drawn and quartered, and his head impaled atop a post. King Edward I, then raided the north with such violence that he was called "the hammer of the Scots".

☛ In 1314, the Scottish hero Robert the Bruce defeated Edward II and led his followers into the northern English counties, looting, burning, and destroying the countryside.

☛ Edward III (1327-77) took his revenge by systematically destroying the Scottish lowlands as far north as Edinburgh. The act of savagery led to new atrocities by the Scots, and new expeditions by England's Richard II (1377-99) and Henry IV (1399-1413).

☛ Through the 15th century, North Britain was reduced to anarchy: Scotland's James I (1406-37) was assassinated by his own henchmen; James II (1437-60) was blown to pieces while attacking the English at Roxburgh; James III (1460-88) was murdered by a family of rampaging border warlords; and James IV (1488-1513 died fighting the English on Flodden Field.

☛ English vengence reached its bloody climax when Henry VIII (1509-47) ordered the ruin of hundreds of border villages in retribution.

☛ The border fell quiet in 1567, when James VI became King of Scotland, and later King of England as well. But in the reign of Charles I, English and Scots went to war again, and hostilities continued during the Cromwell era as well.

☛ Major raids and border risings occurred in 1680, 1689, 1715, and 1745.

☛ For over 700 years, until after 1745, the region never had fifty consecutive years without war.

covered with thatch, called "cabbins." Although building materials were plentiful in the region, the idea of building a permanent house of stone masonry was out of the question. If a war came, it would only be destroyed. Living in the borderlands brought a kind of expediency to everything they did. A family could rebuild a farmhouse quickly if the need came. The house was built in a specific manner, never more than 16-1/2 feet in length (one rod) and consisted of one room with a makeshift fireplace at one end, which was a framed wooden opening coated with clay. All family members slept together on the floor. If the size of the family increased and more room was needed, another cabin would be built next to the first, with a common roof and a breezeway between them.

For centuries these stuctures were the typical homes of the borderers of Scotland and England. It is not surprising that these same structures were to become the main mode of house construction in the Ulster counties of Ireland after large groups of borderers moved there. They were also the dwellings in the backcountry areas of America where the borderers later migrated. The familiar log cabin of the American frontier became a common sight in western Pennsylvania, as well as in the Appalachian settlements stretching from western Maryland and Virginia to the Piedmont region of the Carolinas.

Banishment of the Borderers

A revolutionary change in the culture of the borderers began in the early part of the 18th century, with the Act of Union in 1707. The unification of Scotland and England was to become the beginning of the end for the borderers' way of life. The pacification of the borderlands included the building of gallows to execute the lawless clans or forcibly removing whole clans to Ireland. The old border clan warlords were deprived of their income and fell deep in debt, losing their properties to the merchants of expanding towns. A romantic account of their fate was the history of the Osbaldistone family, in Scott's great border novel, *Rob Roy.*

The old warrior landlords were replaced by a new class of entrepreneurs who saw the future of their region in commerce and coal. Arable lands along the border passed into the hands of agricultural capitalists, mostly from the south of England, and most of whom never set foot on their properties. Systematically, many of the tenants on both sides of the border were either executed or evicted from the land their families had held for centuries. The need for warriors had ended.

The new land owners began building stone walls for the containment of cattle and sheep, a more profitable business than sharecrop farming. The border clans resisted with numerous battles, and by destroying stone fences, roads, or anything that was changing their way of life. But they were fighting a losing battle against the pacification of the borderlands. By the middle of the 18th century, most of the clans were dispersed or had been removed to northern Ireland.

The borderers who were removed to the Ulster counties of Ireland fared no better. The English landlords there were exploiting the tenants with ever increasing rents. A failed crop might mean total ruin to a family because they lived a day-to-day existence with little food, little surplus, and little hope. For the same reasons the borderers were evicted from their traditional homelands in southern Scotland and northern England, they again were evicted from northern Ireland.

Meanwhile, in the early 1700s the descendants of the first "Scotch-Irish" families who had relocated to northern Ireland in the early 1600s were at the end of their 100-year lease period. This gave the English landlords an opportunity to remove a family from the land and replace them at higher rents to newly imported workers from the border region. The English landlords had little sympathy for the plight of the Scotch-Irish workers they were throwing off the land. By 1717 displaced borderers saw the New World as their only hope and refuge. A mass migration to America began. This revolutionary change in culture in the borderlands and northern Ireland took place during most of the 1700s and was the primary reason for the mass migration of the borderers to America.

Northern Ireland by 1715

The Scottish lowlanders transplanted to northern Ireland were mostly Presbyterian with a smattering of Catholics, while the northern British borderers were mostly Anglican Protestants. On each side of the border both groups had a tendancy towards what was called "New Light" Christianity in the 18th century. In Scotland, these New Light Presbyterians were quite numerous on the edges of the Irish Sea. Both the Scot and Briton borderers believed in similar doctrines. Well before moving to Ireland or emigrating to America, both groups had formed the habit of gathering in field meetings and prayer societies.

Northern Ireland today is still the scene of battles between the majority Protestants and minority Catholics. However, the population mix is reversed in the southern region, today the Republic of Ireland, where Catholics are in the majority, and their ethnic origins are primarily Celtic. These religious differences and origins go back to an era when three groups of people divided up the northern part of Ireland.

The groups in northern Ireland in 1715, just prior to the mass migration to America were as follows:

1. **Native Irish.** These people belonged to the ancient Celtic race of Indo-European origin and spoke Gaelic. Celtic is the primary ethnic origin of the highland Scots, southern Irish, Welsh cottagers, Cornish miners,

and natives of the Isle of Man. In northern Ireland, these people were mostly Catholic. After 1700 and the arrival of transplanted Scottish and British borderers, the native Celts of northern Ireland became a minority in their own land.

2. **Scottish Borderers.** These people spoke English and were transplanted from the lowlands of Scotland. They were nearly all "New Light" Presbyterians.

3. **English Borderers.** These were the "New Light" Anglicans transplanted from the northern England border counties to Ireland. They were difficult to tell apart from the Scottish borderers in speech or demeanor.

Borderers to America

"In the summer of 1717, Quaker merchants in Philadelphia noticed that immigrant ships were arriving in more than their usual numbers. By September, the Delaware River was crowded with vessels. They came not from London or Bristol, but from Liverpool and Belfast, and small northern outports with strange-sounding names — Londonderry and Carrickfergus in northern Ireland, Kirkcudbright and Wigtown in Scotland, and Whitehaven and Morecambe on the northern border of England."[6] In October of that year, a Philadelphia Quaker named Jonathan Dickinson complained that the streets of his city were teeming with "a swarm of people... strangers to our Laws and Customs, and even to our Language."[7]

These new immigrants dressed in outlandish ways. The men were tall and lean, with hard, weather-beaten faces. They wore felt hats, loose sackcloth shirts close-belted at the waist, baggy trousers, thick yarn stockings, and wooden shoes. The young women startled Quaker Pennsylvanians by the sensuous appearance of their full bodies, tight waists, bare legs, and skirts considered scandalously short by the Quakers. The speech of these immigrants was English, but they spoke with a slow cadence that rang strangely in the ear. Many were desperately poor. But, even in their poverty, they carried themselves with a fierce and stubborn pride that warned others to treat them with respect.[8]

The first slow trickle of emigration from Ireland to America had actually begun much earlier. In the 17th century, for example, Virginia headgrants had been issued for Irish servants as early as 1630 and a few Irish Calvinists left Belfast for New England in 1636. Both Maryland and Virginia had a few Irish immigrants in the late 17th and early 18th centuries but not without protest from the protestant leadership in these colonies. In my personal family research, I came across a reference to the unwanted Irish in Maryland. My immigrant ancestor to America was Francis Dollahide, a colonial legislator of Maryland. Francis was an English "second son," and an emigrant from Ireland himself in 1680. He once introduced a bill in the Lower House "laying an imposition on the importation (of) too great a number of Irish Papists into this Province."[9] Similarly, in South Carolina, a law of 1716 forbid "what is commonly called native Irish, or persons of known scandalous character, or Roman Catholics."[10] Clearly, the migration of southern Catholic Irish to America was to wait until the middle of the 19th Century.

But the movement of protestant borderers to America began slowly in 1717 - 1718, building to peak periods in 1729, 1741, 1755, 1767, and 1774. It was no coincidence that these peak years were the same as the years of the worst crop failures in northern Ireland. Well over half of the traffic was concentrated in the decade from 1765 to 1775.

During the long period from 1718 to 1775, the annual number of emigrants from Ireland, Scotland, and the north of England averaged about 5,000 a year.[11] It was mainly a migration of families. One British study

estimated that 61 percent of emigrants from northern England traveled in family groups. From the border counties of Scotland, 73 percent were found to be in family groups. This is in comparison with the movement of English immigrants to the Chesapeake region, where the number who came in family groups was as low as seven percent — since the majority of the immigrants in that region were indentured servants.

Unlike the Pilgrims, Puritans, or Quakers, the Scotch-Irish did not come to America for some holy experiment in religious living. Among the borderers there was no talk of a "city upon a hill" as was the case with the East Anglian Puritans. These new emigrants came mainly in search of economic freedom, not religous freedom. They came to find a better life. As former residents of an area of Ireland, England, and Scotland that was ravaged with poor and disposessed people, they were united in their complaints about high rents, low wages, heavy taxes, and short leases. For example, in one study of various sources for the motives in 1719 for emigration from northern Ireland and North Briton, explanations were given as "*Famine, High Rents, Church Taxes, News from America, Short Leases, Little Coin, Luxuries of the Rich, Fall of Linen Trade, Too Little Tillage, and Escape Creditors.*"[12]

In northern Ireland, conditions were so harsh that famine and starvation were often mentioned as the leading cause for migration. At the end of the period, in 1774, four shiploads of immigrants (about 500 persons) were individually asked why they had come to America. Their answers were more positive than before but still strongly materialistic. Once again, they spoke about the greedy landlords, the shortage of food, and their dream of a better life in the New World.[13]

An important stimulus to emigration was correspondence from family and friends who had already made the journey. The attraction of America was felt by all of the border people. Virtually every family was touched by the impact of emigration from these regions. Over half of the populations of northern Ireland, the North Briton borderers, and those from the Scotland border region moved to America during the 18th century.

The process of migration itself had become a big business in the 18th century. The cost of passage for a family had decreased dramatically from the time of migrations to New England, Virginia, or Pennsylvania during the 17th century. Much of the shipping traffic was organized for profit by shipping agents who scoured the countryside in search of likely prospects. Competition for human cargo for the shipping trade caused the fares to go even lower. As a result, the Atlantic crossings passed into the hands of greedy entrepreneurs, with terrible human consequences. Ships were laden beyond their capacity. In 1767 an epidemic broke out on board a crowded emigrant ship bound from Belfast to South Carolina. The unscrupulous owners had packed 450 people into its hold and more than 100 died at sea. Another ship bound from Belfast to Philadelphia ran out of food in mid - passage and forty - six passengers died of starvation. Mortality on ships sailing from Ulster approached that in the slave trade.

When these people arrived in the New World, they faced intense prejudice from other ethnic groups. "I was looked upon as a barbarian," wrote Lieutenant James Mac-Michael.[14] But so desperate were conditions at home that few chose to return to the world they had left. One Scotch-Irish immigrant wrote from Pennsylvania in 1767, "I do not know one that has come here that desires to be in Ireland again." [15]

Quaker leaders pleaded with William Penn to impose restrictions on the numbers of borderers coming into Pennsylvania, but he refused. The Quaker way was one of equality, regardless of a person's ethnic origins. Quaker piety was severely tested by the arrival of the Scotch - Irish in their communities. But, the Quakers found a way to avoid contact with these new immigrants. They banished them to the West.

What is remarkable is that very few of the borderers came to America as indentured servants. Fewer than twenty percent of the northern Irish immigrants were brought to America as servants. Of the lowland Scots and northern Britons, the figure was less than five percent. Part of the reason was that the Scotch-Irish had a reputation of being violent, ungovernable, and very apt to assault their masters. They were not desireable servants. The American colonists had heard tales of rebellions at Barbados and Bermuda where unruly Irish servants had run away, sometimes with the master's wives and daughters in tow.

Yet, the Scotch-Irish who came to America carried a sense of pride in themselves that much irritated the Quakers who couldn't understand what they had to be proud about. It was said of one Scotch-Irish, "His looks spoke out that he would not fear the devil, should he meet him face to face." [16]

Soon after their arrival in Philadelphia and other ports, the borderers were hurried along to wilderness areas. A wagon road as early as the 1730s from Philadelphia via Lancaster, York, and Gettysburg led to the Potomac River and the mouth of the Shenandoah River of Virginia. The Great Valley Road of the Shenandoah Valley became the scene of thousands of Scotch-Irish caravans. Some were calling it "The Irish Road" because of the dominance of the group who used it. After the French-Indian War of 1754-1763, the opening of Forbes' Road through the Appalachian Mountains to the Forks of the Ohio River (now Pittsburgh) became a route which would also be heavily traveled by Scotch-Irish families in pursuit of new homes in the wilderness of southwestern Pennsylvania. In the western regions, the borderers squatted on land that had not been surveyed or even considered ready for farming. These new immigrants did not care much for "civilization," and the idea of moving into virgin wilderness areas suited them perfectly.

Due to the barrier of the Blue Ridge Mountains, a Chesapeake family migrating to the interior of Virginia in the early 1700s had to first travel north to Philadelphia and then south via Lancaster to access the Shenandoah Valley. Another obstacle was the Indians who controlled the area and disliked the white intrusion of their lands. By 1746 a treaty with the Indians gave the whites access to the interior areas. A road was constructed through the Blue Ridge Mountains connecting Alexandria with Winchester, the westernmost town in Virginia at that time. This new "Pioneer's Road" provided a direct route to the Shenandoah Valley from the Chesapeake. As a result, the Potomac River port of Alexandria became an important seaport for incoming Scotch-Irish immigrants.

Borderer Settlements in America

The pattern of moving to the American backcountry was to be followed by the borderers in nearly all of the colonies, from Maine to Georgia. They moved inland to the backwoods and took up land as soon as possible. This was a good solution for the existing colonies along the Atlantic coast of North America as well. For their first 100 years, the American colonies had reasonably good relations with the natives. With some exceptions, Indian wars had not troubled the colonies. But the mountainous inland areas were the domain of more warlike Indian tribes, and the first colonists avoided these areas. It seemed a good place to send the new borderer immigrants. They would make an excellent "buffer zone" between the mountains and the sea and help keep the Indians at bay. History has revealed that the established colonies could not have picked a better group of people to fight their Indian wars for them.

The area of their settlement may be observed in the first census of 1790. The distribution of surnames shows that emigrants from the British-Scottish borderlands found their way into nearly every part of the American colonies. (The exceptions were Rhode Island, Connecticut, and Delaware.) By far the largest concentration was to be found in the backcountry region that included southwestern Pennsylvania, the western parts of Maryland, Virginia, North Carolina, South Carolina, and Georgia. Throughout that broad area, a large majority of the U.S. 1790 population came from Scotland, Ireland, and northern England.

For example, British-Scottish borderers comprised up to 80 percent of the population of Virginia's Augusta, Rockbridge, Fayette, and Lincoln counties. Similar numbers could be seen in Washington County, Pennsylvania. They comprised nearly 100 percent of the population of the Hillsboro district of North Carolina, a large majority in all of South Carolina, and well over half of the entire Georgia population in 1790. They were also the largest group of settlers in the post-1790 states of Kentucky and Tennessee.

Later, the descendants of the borderers would be the dominant group to settle the Old Southwest, an area which today includes the states of Georgia, Alabama, Mississippi, and Louisiana. They also contributed heavily to the number of Americans who went to the Mexican province of Texas in the early 1800s. In the 19th century, Scotch-Irish descendants moved across the Mississippi River to Arkansas, Missouri, Oklahoma, and Texas. By the 20th century, their influence would be felt as far west as New Mexico, Arizona, and southern California.[17]

Speech Patterns: In the United States today, a distinctive dialect of English can still be heard throughout the Appalachian and Ozark Mountains, the lower Mississippi Valley, Texas, and the Southern Plains. It is commonly called "southern highland." This American speech form is over two centuries old. It was recognized in the colonies before the War of Independence and identified at

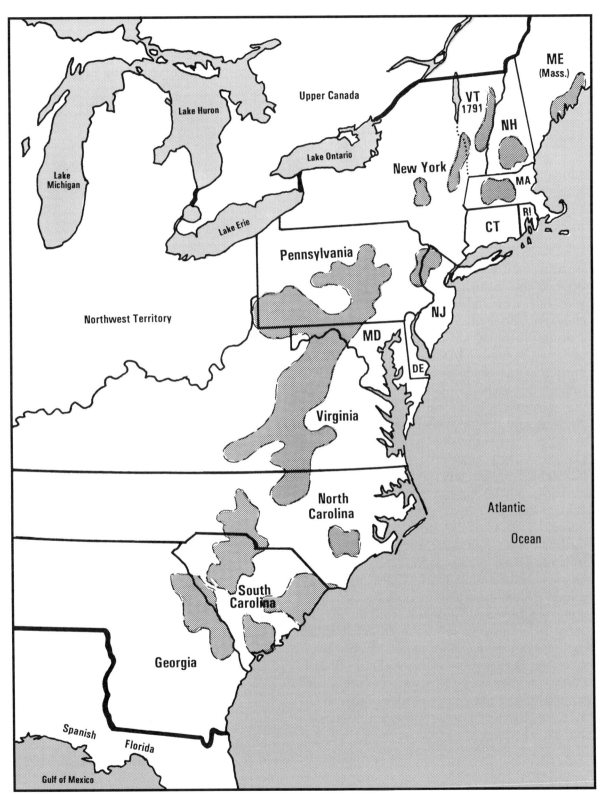

U.S. Settlement areas of the Scottish-British borderers by 1790. Based on a study of the surnames of the 1790 census, a distribution of the so-called "Scotch-Irish" is shown above. The largest region was in the western backcountry of Pennsylvania, Maryland, Virginia, and North Carolina. These immigrants represented over half of the population in both South Carolina and Georgia, as well as substantial pockets of settlements in the northeastern part of the United States.

first in ethnic rather than regional terms as "Scotch-Irish" speech. In the backcountry, it rapidly became so dominant that other ethnic stocks in this region adopted it as their own. As early as 1772, a newspaper advertisement reported a runaway African slave named Jack who was said to "speak the Scotch-Irish dialect." [18] The earliest recorded examples of this "Scotch-Irish" speech were similar to the language that is spoken today. It has become familiar throughout the world as the English of country-western singers, trans-continental truckdrivers, movie cowboys, and backcountry politicians.

Naming patterns: Another common practice of the British and Scottish borderers was the way in which they named their children. The choice for names was different than in other parts of England. Given names included a mix of biblical names, names of border saints, and teutonic names such as Robert or Richard. Popular namesakes in the American backcountry included Saint Andrew, an apostle who became the patron saint of Scotland. A favorite name was David, a name associated not only with its biblical origin but also with a 7th century archbishop who became the patron saint of Wales, and with two early Scottish kings. Patrick was used by both Protestant and Catholic Irish families throughout northern Ireland. These names were rarely found in Quaker, Puritan, or early Chesapeake families. Other examples of borderers' names were Archibald or Ronald, both from the early Scandinavian influence in the border region. Brave warrior names from both sides of the border were Wallace, Bruce, Percy, and Howard. Nostalgic parents even named their children for border places, such as Ross, Clyde, Carlisle, Tyne, Cumberland, and Derry.

A naming rhythm in which every third generation repeated the same name was very similar to the naming pattern found on the Virginia and Maryland plantations. The borderers honored the father's father for a first-born son in a majority of cases. The mother's mother was usually the given name for the first-born daughter.

An example of this naming practice is in the lineage of first-born male descendants in the Taylor family:

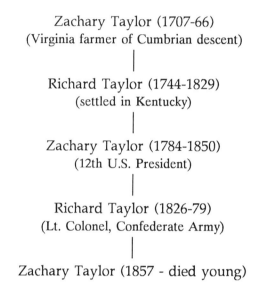

Zachary Taylor (1707-66)
(Virginia farmer of Cumbrian descent)

Richard Taylor (1744-1829)
(settled in Kentucky)

Zachary Taylor (1784-1850)
(12th U.S. President)

Richard Taylor (1826-79)
(Lt. Colonel, Confederate Army)

Zachary Taylor (1857 - died young)

Based on this consistent naming pattern, a genealogist could predict that the first Zachary Taylor's father was probably a Richard Taylor of the Scottish-British borderlands.

The borderers of England and Scotland were a special breed, bringing a special style and culture to America. Many of their traditions and characteristics can still be found in their descendants today. They first came to America's backcountry but were perfectly suited to the challenges of life in the wilderness areas of colonial America. As a people, they had centuries of training in overcoming obstacles of all kinds. And their British, Scottish, and Irish origins reflected a proud, strong-willed, hard working people who contributed greatly to the making of America.

✦ ✦ ✦ ✦ ✦ ✦

NOTES

1. The numbers cited here were based on several works on this subject: Thomas L. Purvis, "The European Ancestry of the United States Population, 1790" in *William and Mary Quarterly,* vol. 85 (1984); James G. Leyburn, *The Scotch-Irish: A Social History,* (Chapel Hill, 1962); Michael Flinn, *Scottish Population History,* (Cambridge, 1977); Ian C. C. Graham, *Colonists from Scotland: Emigration to North America, 1707-1783,* (Ithaca, 1956); Wayland F. Dunaway, *The Scotch-Irish of Colonial Pennsylvania,* (Chapel Hill, 1944); and R. J. Dickson, *Ulster Emigration to Colonial America, 1718-1775,* (London, 1966).

2. Dunaway, *The Scotch-Irish of Colonial Pennsylvania,* p. 10.

3. David Hatcher Fischer, *Albion's Seed: Four British Folkways in America,* (Oxford, 1989), page 605.

4. George M. Fraser, *The Steel Bonnets,* (New York, 1972), p. 66.

5. Ibid, p. 65.

6. Fischer, *Albion's Seed,* p. 622.

7. Letter of Jonathan Dickson to John Aiken, 22 Oct 1717, manuscript in the library of the Historical Society of Pennsylvania.

8. A description of the clothing and bearing of the borderers for that period is in Robert Ferguson, *Northmen in Cumberland and Westmorland,* (London, 1856).

9. "Assembly Proceedings, April 16 - June 3, 1715", *Archives of Maryland,* Vol. 30, p. 64.

10. William A. Schaper, *Sectionalism in South Carolina,* (New York, rpt. 1968), p. 66.

11. Fischer, *Albion's Seed,* p. 608.

12. Dickson, *Ulster Emigration to Colonial America,* p. 46.

13. Ibid, p. 81.

14. "Diary of James MacMichael", in *Pennsylvania Magazine of History and Biography,* Vol. 16 (1892), p. 145.

15. A. C. Davis, "Letter From an Immigrant in Pennsylvania, 1766", in *Pennsylvania History,* Vol. 50 (1983), p. 313.

16. George R. Gilmer, *Sketches of Some of the First Settlers of Upper Georgia,* (Baltimore, 1965), p. 62.

17. Fischer, *Albion's Seed,* p. 634.

18. *Virginia Gazette,* 22 Oct 1772.

Sources for Genealogical Research in Great Britain

In addition to the "British Place-Finding Sources" (see pp 3-6), there are several noteworthy reference books and resources for genealogical research in the England, Wales, Scotland, and Northern Ireland. A selected list of these is shown below:

Research Handbooks and Guides to Records

● Baxter, Angus, *In Search of Your British and Irish Roots.* (Baltimore: Genealogical Publishing Co., Inc., 1991, 310 pages) This is a good handbook to beginning genealogical research in the British Isles.

● Bethell, David, *English Ancestry* (Leek, Straffordshire, England: Melandra Publishers, 1981, 394 pages). This book includes an overview of English research possibilities, plus some excellent maps.

● Campbell, R. G., *Scotch-Irish Family Research Made Simple,* a guide to origins and movements of the borderers of Scotland and England to northern Ireland and to America. The book explains how to conduct research in sources at the Belfast and Dublin Record Offices, public archives, and church records. (Available for $13.50 from AGLL Genealogical Services, PO Box 329, Bountiful, UT 84011).

● Chapman, Colin R., *Tracing Your British Ancestry,* 1993 edition (Available from AGLL Genealogical Services, PO Box 329, Bountiful, UT 84011).

● Chapman, Colin R., *Ecclesiastical Courts, Their Officials and Their Records,* (Available for $16.45 from AGLL Genealogical Services, PO Box 329, Bountiful, UT 84011). This book describes the Ecclesiastical Legal System, the records, and locations.

● Chapman, Colin R., *Pre-1841 Censuses and Population Listings in the British Isles, 1992, 92 pages.* (Available for $16.45 from AGLL Genealogical Services, PO Box 329, Bountiful, UT 84011). Contains information and instructions on extracting genealogical data from early population lists.

● Cory, Kathleen B., *Tracing Your Scottish Ancestry,* contains a step-by-step guide to information on where and how to search records at the New Register House, Scottish Records Offices, and other sources. (Available for $19.45 from AGLL Genealogical Services, PO Box 329, Bountiful, UT 84011).

● Currer-Briggs, Noel, and Royston Gambier, *Debrett's Family Historian: A Guide to Tracing Your Ancestry.* (London: Debrett Webb and Bower, 1881). This is a classic guide to English ancestry.

● Dunn, Phillip B., *A Guide to Ancestral Research in London,* 109 pages, (Available for 16.45 from AGLL Genealogical Services, PO Box 329, Bountiful, UT 84011).

● Durning, Bill and Mary Durning, *The Scotch-Irish Who Came to America: A Genealogical History,* 1997, 238 pages, (La Mesa, CA: The Irish Family Names Society).

Available for $21.45 from AGLL Genealogical Services, PO Box 329, Bountiful, UT 84011). This is a good little book, not for the history, but for locating the places in northern Ireland where a Scotch-Irish family name originates. Over half of the pages give an alphabetized list of Scotch-Irish names keyed to the places in Ireland where the names can be found in the early 1700s.

● Eakle, Arlene H., *Descriptive Inventory of the English Collection,* Salt Lake City: University of Utah Press, 1979, 168 pages). This is a finding aid to the microfilmed manuscript British collection at the Family History Library in Salt Lake City.

● Falley, Margaret D., *Irish and Scotch-Irish Ancestral Research: A Guide to the Genealogical Records, Methods and Sources in Ireland,* 2 volumes, 1988. (Available for $63.50 from AGLL Genealogical Services). Volume 1 identifies repositories and records, volume 2 contains an extensive bibliography and family index.

● FitzHugh, Terrick V. H., *The Dictionary of Genealogy* (Totowa, NJ: Barnes and Noble, 1985, 320 pages).

● Franklin, Charles M., *Welsh Genealogical Research.* This book includes an explanation of the naming system found only in Wales, one of the last countries to adopt surnames. It contains a list of resources unique to Wales, and translations of names and words of use in genealogical seaching. (Available for $17.50 from AGLL Genealogical Services, PO Box 329, Bountiful, UT 84011).

● Gardner, David E., and Frank Smith, *Genealogical Research in England and Wales* (Salt Lake City: Bookcraft Publishers, 1964, 3 vols.).

● Gibson, Jeremy, *A Directory of Holdings in Great Britain Poll Books, 1696-1872,* 60 pages. (Available for $16.45 from AGLL Genealogical Services, PO Box 329, Bountiful, UT 84011). This book lists all known printed and manuscript poll books in public repositories throughout England, Wales, and Scotland. Before 1872, when secret ballot voting was introduced, voting was a public matter, and a record of how people voted was frequently published.

● Gibson, Jeremy, *The Hearth Tax: Other Later Stuart Tax Lists, and the Association Oath Rolls,* 60 pages, (Available for $11.00 from AGLL Genealogical Services, PO Box 329, Bountiful, UT 84011). A description and location of specialized name lists in the British Isles.

● Gibson, Jeremy, *A Simplified Guide to Record Offices in England and Wales,* 57 pages. (Available for $11.00 from AGLL Genealogical Services, PO Box 329, Bountiful, UT 84011).

● Gibson, Jeremy, *Bishops' Transcripts and Marriage Licenses: A Simplified Guide to their Locations and Indexes in England, Wales, and Ireland,* 3rd Edition, 40 pages. (Available for $11.00 from AGLL Genealogical Services, PO Box 329, Bountiful, UT 84011).

● Gibson, Jeremy, *A Simplified Guide to Probate Jurisdictions: Where to Look for Wills in Great Britain and Ireland,* 3rd Edition, 72 pages. (Available for $11.00 from AGLL Genealogical Services, PO Box 329, Bountiful, UT 84011).

● Hanna, Charles A., *The Scotch-Irish: or, The Scot in North Briton, North Ireland, and North America,* 2 volumes. Volume 1 gives a survey of the origins of the Scotch-Irish, and their history. Volume 2 details the migration to America of the Scotch-Irish. (Available for $78.50 from AGLL Genealogical Services, PO Box 329, Bountiful, UT 84011).

● Irvine, Shirley, *Your English Ancestry: A Guide for North Americans,* 1993, 196 pages. (Available for $15.50 from AGLL Genealogical Services, PO Box 329, Bountiful, UT 84011.

● Irvine, Shirley, *Your Scottish Ancestry: A Guide for North Americans,* 1994, 386 pp.

(Available for $15.50 from AGLL Genealogical Services, PO Box 329, Bountiful, UT 84011.

● Konrad, J., *English Family Research*, (1989, 65 pages). Available for $11.50 from AGLL Genealogical Services, PO Box 329, Bountiful, UT 84010.

● Leese, Anna T., *Blood Royal: Issue of the Kings and Queens of Medieval England, 1066-1399*, 1996, 468 pages. (Available for $40.50 from AGLL Genealogical Services, PO Box 329, Bountiful, UT 84011).

● Mellen, Rachel, *The Handy Book to English Genealogy*, 3rd edition, 1990, 228 pages, available for $20.50 from AGLL Genealogical Services, PO Box 329, Bountiful, UT 84011.

● Moody, David, *Scottish Local History: An Introductory Guide*, 1989, 178 pages. (Available for $22.45 from AGLL Genealogical Services, PO Boxs 329, Bountiful, UT 84011).

● Moody, David, *Scottish Family History*, a guide to Scottish archives, libraries, and record offices. (Available for $22.45 from AGLL Genealogical Services, PO Box 329, Bountiful, UT 84011).

● Moulton, Joy W., *Genealogical Resources in English Repositories*, 1996, with supplement, 648 pages. (Available for $48.50 from AGLL Genealogical Services, PO Box 329, Bountiful, UT 84011). This is a comprehensive review of sources available in English libraries, archives, and county record houses. Records available in the U.S. are identified, along with addresses for the various repositiories..

● Owen, Dolores B., *Guide to Genealogical Sources in the British Isles*, (Metuchen, NJ: The Scarecrow Press, Inc., 1989, 409 pages). This book identifies in alphabetical order, virtually every county record office, national library, archives, and other repositiories in England, Wales, Scotland, and northern Ireland, along with their address and phone numbers. It describes what each facility contains in relation to genealogical material.

● Pelling, George, *Beginning Your Family History in Great Britain*, 4th Edition, 1987, 64 pages. (Available for $10.50 from AGLL Genealogical Services, PO Box 329, Bountiful, UT 84011). This is an easy-to-read overview of what to expect in English genealogical research.

● Reid, Judith R., *Genealogical Research in England's Public Record Office: A Guide for North Americans*, 1996, 164 pages. (Available for $26.00 from AGLL Genealogical Services, PO Box 329, Bountiful, UT 84011). The Public Records Office in London is one of the richest sources for genealogical materials in the world. Its records reach back to the Domesday books of 1086 and forward to a vast accumulation of census records, probate documents, and emigration records that make it a natural magnet for anyone undertaking English or Welsh genealogical research. This book describes the records and how one can access the materials via mail.

● Rowlands, John, ed., *Welsh Family History: A Guide to Research*. Coverage includes Welsh archives, family history societies, parish registers, civil registration, surnames, placenames, the IGI for Wales, wills and estate records, printed and manuscript pedigrees, emigration, and a variety of miscellaneous sources, 1994, 316 pages. (Available for $23.45 from AGLL Genealogical Services, PO Box 329, Bountiful, UT 84011).

● Saul, Pauline, *The Family Historian's Enquire Within*, (London: Federation of Family History Societies, 5th Edition, 1995, 287 pages). This is an outstanding A to Z guide of resources available to genealogists in English repositories. It explains terms and abbreviations, and a description of the types of records available for genealogical pursuits. This is a very thorough and indespensible guidebook for English genealogical research.

● Sinclair, Cecil, *Tracing Scottish Local History*, (Available for $19.45 from AGLL Genealogical Services, PO Box 329, Bountiful, UT 84011).

● Sinclair, Cecil, *Tracing Your Scottish Ancestors in the Public Record Offices*, a survey of records in civil, church, and courts. Explanations are given on searching births and marriages, and a variety of other less-known sources. (Available for $23.50 from AGLL Genealogical Services, PO Box 329, Bountiful, UT 84011).

● Steel, Donald John, *Discovering Your Family History* (London: British Broadcasting Company), 1986, 195 pages).

● Stuart, Roderick and Douglas Richardson, *Royalty for Commoners: The Complete Known Lineage of John of Gaunt, Son of Edward III, King of England, and Queen Philippa*, 1992, 412 pages. (Available for $33.50 from AGLL Genealogical Services, PO Box 329, Bountiful, UT 84011).

Indexes to Family Histories

● Bridger, Charles, *An Index to Printed Pedigrees Contained in County and Local Histories, the Herald's Visitations and in the More Important Genealogical Collections*, (London: J.R. Smith, 1867, 384 pages, reprinted Genealogical Publishing Co., Inc., 1969.

● Marshall, George W., *The Genealogist's Guide*, (Publ. by the author, 1903, 880 pages). This is an index to British pedigrees extracted from hundreds of books printed prior to 1903, continuing the work of Charles Bridger.

● Whitmore, John B., *A Genealogical Guide: An Index to British Pedigrees in Continuation of Marshall's Genealogist's Guide, 1903*, (London: Walford Bros, 1953, 658 pages).

● Barrow, Geoffrey B., *The Genealogist's Guide: An Index to Printed British Pedigrees and Family Histories, 1950-1975*. (American Library Association, 1977). Barrow continues the index to printed family histories, begun by Bridger, Marshall, and Whitmore.

● Thomson, Theodore R., *A Catalogue of British Family Histories*, (London: Research Pub. Co., for the Society of Genealogists, regularly updated).

● Stuart, Margaret, *Scottish Family History: A Guide to Works of Reference on the History and Genealogy of Scottish Families*. This guidebook is comparable to the Marshall *Genealogist's Guide* for English family histories — a time-saving and comprehensive guide to family histories contained in books, pamphlets, periodicals, and manuscript collections. (Available for $28.50 from AGLL Genealogical Services, PO Box 329, Bountiful, UT 84011).

Bibliographies

● Filby, William P., *American and British Genealogy and Heraldry: A Selected List of Books*, 3rd edition, (Boston: New England Historic Genealogical Society, 1983, 736 pages).

● Gatfield, George, *Guide to Printed Books and Manuscripts Relating to English and Foreign Heraldry and Genealogy*, (London: Mitchell & Hughes, 1892, 646 pages, reprinted by Gale Research of Detroit, Michigan, 1966, and later)

● Humphrey-Smith, Cecil R., *A Genealogist's Bibliography*, (Baltimore: Genealogical Publishing Co., 1966, 128 pages).

Guides & Indexes to Parish Registers

● *Parish and Vital Records List*, published several times per year by the Family History Library of The Church of Jesus Christ of Latter-day Saints. The *Parish and Vital Records List* shows which world-wide records have been indexed and listed in the *International Genealogical Index (IGI)* for each geographical area and time period. It also shows which records are currently being extracted. The IGI is updated periodically and is organized by country. For the British Isles, the IGI is the most comprehensive index to Parish Registers available anywhere.

● *Index to Church of Scotland Parish Records,* (Old Parochial Registers Index for Scotland). Over 10 million names are in this index to all of Scotland's Presbyterian parishes from the 1500s through 1854. The index is available on microfilm at the Family History Library in Salt Lake City, and was recently added to the "Family Search" computer system. As an index, one can use this listing to locate a particular parish in Scotland where a surname occurs. Virtually all of the Scottish parish records have been microfilmed.

● Bloxham, V. B., *Key to the Parochial Registers of Scotland: From Earliest Times Through 1854,* This is the standard reference to the 900 parochial registers of Scotland. It is also a complete guide to the parish records on microfilm at the Family History Library in Salt Lake City.

● *The Challen Parish Register Typescripts.* This series of microfilms includes actual parish records from London, the Midlands counties, and the southern counties of England. A copy is at the Library of Congress in Washington, DC and the Family History Library in Salt Lake City, Utah.

● *Parish Registers: A Handlist.* (London: Corporation of London Library Committee, 2 vols.

● Humphrey-Smith, Cecil R., *The Phillimore Atlas and Index of Parish Registers,* (Baltimore: Genealogical Publishing Co., Inc., 1984, 282 pages, reprinted by Phillimore Publishers, 1995). These are the most definitive maps available showing the parishes within each county of England, Wales, Scotland, and northern Ireland. In addition to the maps, a list by each county itemizes what parish records are extant, which have had names indexed in the International Genealogical Index (IGI), Boyd's Index, plus any other published indexes to parish records by any known party. As a tool for British research, there is

probably no other book of equal importance.

● Steel, Donald J., *National Index of Parish Registers,* 3rd edition, 13 vols. (Published for the Society of Genealogists by Phillimore). This is the most comprehensive guide to Anglican, Roman Catholic and nonconformist registers before 1837, together with information on marriage licenses, Bishop's transcripts, and modern copies.

● Timmons, Sylvia A., *Printed English and Welsh Parish Registers in the George Peabody Branch, Enoch Pratt Free Library, Baltimore, Maryland,* (Baltimore: Genealogical Publ. Co., Inc., 1979, 104 pages).

Local History & Biography

● Emmison, Frederick G., *Archives and Local History,* (Phillimore, 1974, 112 pages).

● Humphreys, Arthur Lee, *A Handbook to County Biography: Being A Bibliography of Bibliographies Relating to the Counties and Towns of Great Britain and Ireland,* (London: Strangeways and Son, 1917, 501 pages; reprinted in 1974 by Dawsons, London).

● Stephens, W. B., *Sources for English Local History,* (Cambridge: Cambridge University Press, 1981, 342 pages). This book is an academic text which identifies the sources of history and studies in the use of historical evidence.

● Pugh, Ralph Bernard, *The Victoria History of the Counties of England.* (London: published for the Institute of Historical Research by Oxford University Press, 1970, 282 pages). This is a guide to the Victoria histories of the counties of England representing scholarly local history research. Begun around 1900, this project has published local history volumes for about a third of the English counties. Among the subjects are the Domesday Books, bibliographies, eminent persons, maps, topographical accounts of parishes and manors, parish histories (including religious houses) and descriptions of hospitals, industries, schools, and sports. The volumes for the completed counties are valuable resources. Each county volume is probably the best overall review of English towns and parishes, particularly for their history. Microfilm copies of all the Victoria County Histories in print are available through the Family History Library in Salt Lake City.

● West, John, *Town Records,* Chichester, Sussex (Phillimore, 1983, 366 pages). This is a guide to town records in England, what to expect, and how to go about locating the records.

● West, John, *Village Records,* (London: Macmillan; New York: St. Martin's Press, 1962, 208 pages). This is a guide to village records in England, similar to West's guidebook on town records.

● *Crockford's Clerical Directory,* (London: Oxford University Press, 1858).

● Stephens, Leslie and Sidney Lee, *Dictionary of National Biography,* (London: Smith, Elder, 1885-1901).

● *Who Was Who: A Companion to Who's Who, Containing the Biographies of Those Who Died,* (London: A. & C. Black, 1897-1917.

● *The British Biographical Archive,* microfiche, (Available at the Library of Congress, Washington, DC), this is a copy of 384 of the most important English language biographical reference works published between 1601 and 1929. Included are some 240,000 persons of local, regional, national, and international importance from England, Scotland, Wales, and Ireland.

● *British and Irish Biographies, 1840-1940,* microfiche, (Available at the Library of Congress, Washington, DC), lists information from 273 biographical dictionaries published between 1840 and 1940. Included are general biographical collections, with an index to more than 180,000 prominent and not-so-prominent British and Irish persons.

Maps, Atlases, Gazetteers & Placenames

● Gardner, David E., *A Genealogical Atlas of England and Wales,* (Salt Lake City: Deseret Book Co., 1960).

● Lewis, Samuel, *A Topographical Dictionary of England, Comprising the Several Counties, Cities, Boroughs, Corporate and Market Towns, Parishes, and Townships, and the Islands of Guernsey, Jersey, and Man, With Historical and Statistical Descriptions,* (London: S. Lewis and Co., 1844, four volumes). Reprints of this gazetteer have been printed by various publishers over the years. It is simply the best overall listing of English places. The four volumes are available on microfiche for $20.00 each, (Vol 1. Aab-Cwm, Vol. 2. Dag-Kyr, Vol. 3. Lad-Ryt, and Vol. 4. Sad-Zen), or all four volumes on microfiche for $68.00) from AGLL Genealogical Services, PO Box 329, Bountiful, UT 84011.

● Lewis, Samuel, *A Topographical Dictionary of Scotland,* similar to the English version, this is an 1851 publication which lists virtually every place in Scotland, including parishes, villages, towns, etc. The parish for every place is given, making this list a place-finding tool. The two volumes are available as hardbound books for $75.00, microfiche for $16.00, or vol. 1 (Abbo-Jura) for $10.00, and vol. 2 (Keig-Zetl) for $10.00 from AGLL Genealogical Services, PO Box 329, Bountiful, UT 84011.

● Lewis, Samuel, *A Topographical Dictionary of Wales,* similar to the English and Scottish versions, this is an 1834 publication which lists virtually every place in Wales, including parishes, villages, towns, etc. The parish for every place is given, making this list a place-finding tool. The two volumes are available on microfiche for $22.50, or vol. 1 (Abb-Kni) for $12.00, and vol. 2 (Lam-Yva) for $15.00 from AGLL Genealogical Services, PO Box 329, Bountiful, UT 84011.

● Mitchell, Brian, *A New Genealogical At-*

las of Ireland, (Available for $22.45 from AGLL Genealogical Services, PO Box 329, Bountiful, UT 84011).

● Smith, Frank, *A Genealogical Gazetteer of England: An Alphabetical Dictionary of Places, with the Location, Ecclesiastical Jurisdiction, Population, and the Date of the Earliest Entry in the Registers of Every Ancient Parish in England.* (Baltimore: Genealogical Publishing Co., Inc., 1968, 599 pages, available for $38.50 from AGLL Genealogical Services, PO Box 329, Bountiful, UT 84011).

● *Ordnance Survey Maps of Great Britain.* These are county maps, at a scale of six inches to the mile, which reflect the area in the mid to late nineteenth century, showing manor houses, castles, etc. The maps are indexed by county. Survey maps exist for England, Wales, and Scotland. There are also thousands of single sheet maps of Great Britain, which show estates, coats of arms, cities, and towns. These are the most detailed large scale maps and the best for genealogical purposes. A complete set of these maps is available at only a few major libraries in the U.S., e.g., the Library of Congress and the Family History Library in Salt Lake City.

● *U.S. Defense Department Gazetteers,* available at major University Map Libraries in the U.S., these computer-generated lists show a placename and a latitude-longitude location. Gazetteers exist for virtually every country of Europe. The placenames were extracted from the U.S. Army Mapping Service maps. These maps were created at a scale of 1:24,000 and primarily used for military purposes. The maps themselves are not sold to the public. But, the placename lists taken from the detailed maps are special publications that can be viewed at a map library.

● Cameron, Kenneth, *English Place-names,* (London: B.T. Batsford, 1977, 3rd Ed., 258 pages).

● Ekwall, Eilert, *The Concise Oxford Dictionary of English Place-names,* (Oxford: Clarendon Press, 1960, 4th ed., 546 pages).

● Reaney, Percy H., *The Origin of English Place-names,* (London: Routledge and Paul, 1960, 277 pages).

Surnames

● Bardsley, Charles, *A Dictionary of English and Welsh Surnames: With Special American Instances,* London, New York: H. Frowde, 1901, 837 pages, reprinted by Genealogical Publishing Co., Inc., Baltimore, 1967).

● Ewen, Cecil, *A History of the Surnames of the British Isles: A Concise Account of their Origin, Evolution, Etymology, and Legal Status,* (London: K. Paul Trench, Trubner, Ltd, 1931, 508 pages). A "Short Bibliography" (pages 429-36) was reprinted by Gale Research of Detroit and Genealogical Publishing Company of Baltimore in 1968.

● Reaney, Percy H., *The Origins of English Surnames,* (New York: Barnes and Noble, 1967, 415 pages).

● Rowlands, John and Sheila Rowlands, *The Surnames of Wales.* The book includes over 40 maps showing the incidence and distribution of surnames in Wales, 1996, 217 pages. (Available for $23.45 from AGLL Genealogical Services, PO Box 329, Bountiful, UT 84011).

● *The Norman People and their Existing Descendants in the British Dominions and the United States of America,* (London: H.S. King & Co., 1874, reprinted by Genealogical Publishing Co., Inc., 1975). This is an alphabetical listing of Norman names taken from Post Office directories.

● Goss, Charles, *The London Directories, 1677-1855: A Bibliography With Notes on their Origin and Development,* London: D. Archer, 1932, 146 pages).

● Norton, Jane E., *Guide to the National and Provincial Directories of England and Wales,* (London: Royal Historical Society, 1950, 241 pages).

The Domesday Book

The *Domesday Book* is the record of William the Conqueror's survey of England in 1086. For the majority of English villages and towns, the book is the starting point of their recorded history. It is organized by county. This is the first English census, considered by some as the most remarkable administrative accomplishment of the Middle Ages. It provides a record of English social organization in the Anglo-Norman period. The works listed below attempt to assist modern reseachers who want to consult the book.

● Burk, John B., ed., *The Roll of Battle Abbey*, (Baltimore: 'Genealogical Publishing Co., Inc., 1978, 107 pages).

● Morris, John, ed., *Domesday Book*, the text and translation, (Chichester: Phillimore, 1986, 39 volumes.

● Hinde, Thomas, ed., *The Domesday Book*, (New York: Crown, 1985, 351 pages).

● Ellis, Henry, Sir, *A General Introduction to Domesday Book: Accompanied by Indexes of the Tenants-in-chief, and Under-tenants, at the Time of the Survey; as Well as the Holders of Lands Mentioned in Domesday Anterior to the Formation of the Record; with an Abstract of the Population of England at the Close of the Reign of William the Conqueror, so Far as the Same is Actually Entered*, (London: G. Eyre & A. Spottiswoode, 1833, 2 volumes, reprinted by Genealogical Publishing Co., Inc., Baltimore, 1971).

The Royal Commission

The **Royal Commsission on Historical Manuscripts** acts as a clearing house for information about the nature and location of historical papers outside of England's Public Record Office. It is located at Quality Court, Chancery Lane, London, WC2A 1HP. The Commission maintains a large computer database for locating repositiories for manu-

scripts in Great Britain. There is no surname index. The database contains information about various manuscripts, what they contain, and where they are physically located in Great Britain. A review of the records that can be located through the Royal Commission are shown below along with a few guides that have been produced about the records:

● *Manorial Documents Register.* The Royal Commission on Historical Manuscripts (RCHM) maintains a list of manors in England and their surviving records. It also maintains a registry of *Manor Court Rolls.* By writing to the RCHM, a researcher can learn which manors were in a given parish in England and where the old records of these manors may be found, if they survive. The Manor Court Rolls are identified by the name of the Lord of the Manor, and then by the location of that manor within a county and parish. It is in the manor records and court rolls that the home of an early English ancestor may be found, showing their residence even before 1550. If an ancestor were a tenant farmer, he was essentially "under contract" with a particular Lord and Manor. While under the Lord's jurisdiction, he was subject to the Lord's Court, where matters of his tenancy were recorded, as well as any other matter of interest to the tenant and Lord. The Manor Documents often include vital information about the tenants, including births, marriages, and deaths. The original documents generated by the manor courts are stored today mostly in county record houses all over Britain. Although they contain a wealth of information, one must know in advance the name of the Lord of the Manor before these records can be used. The location of the manors can usually be determined if the name of the parish is known. Manor bounds did not coincide with those of a parish. Any one parish might include portions of several manors. Therefore, once a parish has been determined for an English ancestor, the next step is to determine if the ancestor was a tenant farmer on a manor within that parish.

● Park, Peter, *My Ancestors Were Manorial Tenants: How Can I Find Out More About Them?* (London: Society of Genealogists, 1994).

● Palgrave-Moore, *How to Locate and Use Manorial Records,* (London: Federation of Family History Societies).

Religions

● Jackson, Ronald V., *Inventory of Church Records of the British Isles,* (Bountiful, UT; Accelerated Indexing Systems, 1976, 109 pages).

● Lart, Charles Edmund, *Huguenot Pedigress,* (London: The St. Catherine Press, 1925, 2 volumes. Reprinted by Genealogical Publishing Co., Inc., Baltimore, 1967).

● Rosenstein, Neil, *The Unbroken Chain: Biographical Sketches and the Genealogy of Illustrious Jewish Families from the 15th-20th Century,* (New York: Shengold Publishers, 1976, 716 pages).

Wills

● Camp, Anthony J., *Wills and their Whereabouts: Being a Thorough Revision and Extension of the Previous Work of the Same Name by B. G. Bouwens,* (Canterbury: published for the Society of Genealogists by Phillimore, 1963, 137 pages).

● Gibson, Jeremy S., *A Simplified Guide to Probate Jurisdictions: Where to Look for Wills in Great Britain and Ireland,* (Baltimore: Genealogical Publishing Co., Inc., 1986, 62 pages).

● Gibson, Jeremy S., *Wills and Where to Find Them,* (Baltimore: Genealogical Publishing Co., Inc., 1974, 210 pages.

● *A List of Wills, Administrations, Etc., in the Public Record Office, London, England, 12th-19th Century,* (Baltimore: Genealogical Publishing Co., Inc., 1968, 158 pages).

British Materials on Microfilm at the Library of Congress

Since 1905 the Library of Congress has been copying materials in British archives, libraries, and the Public Record Office (PRO) that relate to American history. For example, the Library of Congress has PRO records of individuals and families emigrating to America; original correspondence regarding America and the West Indies; and documents regarding American Loyalists. All of the microfilmed English materials relating to America can be used through interlibrary loan. Arrangements for interlibrary loan should be made through a local library. The Library of Congress has guides to these microfilmed records which can be consulted at their Manuscript Reading Room.

● *Public Record Office Genealogy,* a Selection of Leaflets, published by the PRO.

● Griffin, Grace Gardner, *A Guide to Manuscripts Relating to American History in British Depositories* describes British documents at the Library of Congress acquired before 1944.

● *Manuscripts on Microfilm: A Checklist of the Holdings in the Manuscript Division.* this is a description of Library of Congress holdings acquired from 1944 to 1976.

● *The British Manuscripts Project* includes manuscripts from the Cambridge University Library, the Public Record Office (including the Colonial Office) Lincoln Cathedral, Oxford University (Bodleian Library), the National Library of Wales, and several other libraries, such as Longleat, Holkham hall, Penshurst, Knole, Woburn Abbey, and Syon House. An index to the collection is Lester K. Born's *British Manuscripts Project, A Checklist of the Microfilms Prepared in England and Wales for the American Council of Learned Societies, 1941 - 1945.* The index and the manuscripts can be viewed at the Microform Reading Room at the Library of Congress, and are available on interlibrary loan to a local library.

● *National Inventory of Documentary Sources in the United Kingdom* is a list of published and unpublished finding aids for archive and manuscript collections in the United Kingdom. It does not provide copies of the records themselves. The scope of this project includes description of materials in county record offices (Berkshire, Gloucester, Bristol, Essex), university and public libraries, (Bodleian) and special and private repositories (Guildhall Library, National Library of Wales). The Library of Congress guide No. 101 describes the inventory.

● *Records of the States of the United States of America* ("Early State Records") includes local, county, and city records, as well as newspapers for British colonial America. Legislative, stautory law, constitutional, administrative, executive, and court records are indexed. The records are described in *A Guide to the Microfilm Collection of Early State Records* prepared by the Library of Congress.

Emigrants from Great Britain to the American Colonies

● Thompson, Roger, *Mobility and Migration: East Anglian Founders of New England, 1629-1640.* (Amherst, MA: University of Massachusetts Press, 1994, 305 pages.)

● Anderson, Robert Charles, *The Great Migration Begins: Immigrants to New England, 1620-1633.* (2 volumes). This is the first publication resulting from a survey to identify each of the approximately 22,000 original Pilgrim and Puritan immigrants to New England from 1620 to 1643. Each immigrant during that period will be given a biographical sketch, along with the person's origins in Great Britain, and genealogical notes for each relating to their descendants in America and their families in England. The project was created by the New England Historic Genealogical Society

(NEHGS). The first two volumes were published in 1995 covering the arrivals between 1620 and 1633, and has information on some 900 families plus unattached individuals, with over 2,500 persons total. A third volume was published in 1997. These publications are available only from the NEHGS, 101 Newbury St., Boston, MA 02116.

● Banks, Charles E., *The English Ancestry and Homes of the Pilgrim Fathers Who Came to Plymouth Colony on the "Mayflower" in 1620, the "Fortune" in 1621, and the "Anne" and the "Little James" in 1623,* (reprinted, Baltimore: Genealogical Publishing Co., Inc., 1968, 187 pages).

● Banks, Charles E., *The Winthrop Fleet of 1630: An Account of the Vessels, the Voyage, the Passengers and their English Homes from Original Authorities,* (Originally published 1930, reprinted by Genealogical Publishing Co., Inc., Baltimore, 1989).

● Banks, Charles E., *Topographical Dictionary of 2,285 English Emigrants to New England, 1620-1650* identifies emigrants, giving their English homes, names of ships in which they sailed, and reference to the printed or manuscript sources from which the information was derived. This is a classic work on Puritans to America and from which the English origins of the Puritans to New England can be precisely identified. (Available for $28.50 from AGLL Genealogical Services, PO Box 329, Bountiful, UT 84011).

● Banks, Charles E., *The Planters of the Commonwealth,* (Available for $23.50 from AGLL Genealogical Services, PO Box 329, Bountiful, UT 84011). This books lists the names of passengers of ninety-six ships that came to New England from 1620-1640. The name of the ship, ship's captain, and where known, the passengers' English origins and place of settlement in New England. This is very authoratative and useful book for the identification of the Puritans and their means of transportation to New England during the Great Migration.

● Farmer, John, *A Genealogical Register of the First Settlers of New England,* 1929, 1994, (Available for $28.50 from AGLL Genealogical Services, PO Box 329, Bountiful, UT 84011). This book Identifies immigrants admitted to the Massachusetts Bay Colony from 1630-1662 and many of the early inhabitants of New England, Long Island, and New York from 1620 to 1675.

● Savage, James, *A Genealogical Dictionary of the First Settlers of New England, Showing Three Generations of Those Who Came Before May 1692,* 4 volumes, 2,541 pages, originally published in 1860, reprinted 1994 by Genealogical Publishing Co., Baltimore. (Available for $128.50 from AGLL Genealogical Services, PO Box 329, Bountiful, UT 84011). The early settlers are identified by name, birth, marriage, death, children, birth and death of children, and birthdates of grandchildren. A genealogy cross-index is included. This is a standard work on New England genealogy, and includes most of the earliest English immigrants to New England.

● Hotten, John C., *Our Early Emigrant Ancestors: The Original List of Persons of Quality, Emigrants, Religious Exiles, Political Rebels, Serving Men Sold For a Term of Years, Apprentices, Children Stolen, Maidens Pressed, and Others Who Went from Great Britain to the American Plantations, 1600-1700, With Their Ages, the Localities Where They Formerly Lived in the Mother Country, the Names of the Ships in Which They Embarked and Other Interesting Particulars.* (reprinted 1968, Baltimore: Genealogical Publishing Co., Inc., 580 pages). This book is the definitive study of the earliest emigrants from England to Virginia and Maryland and is commonly referred to as "Hotten's List."

● Brandow, James C., *Omitted Chapters From Hotten's Original Lists of Persons of Quality and Others Who Went From Great Britain to the American Plantations, 1600-1700,* adds 6,000 entries of emigrants to the Virginia and Maryland plantations, taken from British public records. 245 pages. (Available for $23.50 from AGLL Genealogical Services, PO Box 329, Bountiful, UT 84011).

● Greer, George Cabell, *Early Virginia Immigrants, 1623-1666,* (Baltimore: Genealogical Publishing Co., Inc., 1960, 376 pages).

● Newman, Harry Wright, *To Maryland From Overseas,* (Annapolis, MD: H.W. Newman, 1982, 190 pages).

● Hargreaves - Mawdsley, R., *Bristol and America, A Record of the First Settlers in the Colonies of North America, 1654-1685: Including the Names with Places of Origin of More Than 10,000 Servants to Foreign Plantations who Sailed from the Port of Bristol to Virginia, Maryland, and Other Parts of the Atlantic Coast, and Also the West Indies, from 1654 to 1685.* (A new 182-page edition was printed in 1967, edited by Peter Colham, and published by Genealogical Publishing Co. of Baltimore).

● Coldham, Peter Wilson, *The Complete Book of Emigrants, 1607-1660: A Comprehensive Listing Compiled from English Public Records of Those Who Took Ship to the Americas for Political, Religious, and Economic Reasons; and of Those Who Were Sold to Labour in the New Colonies,* (Baltimore: Genealogical Publishing Co., Inc., 1987, 600 pages).

● Coldham, Peter Wilson, *The Complete Book of Emigrants in Bondage, 1614-1775,* Vol. 1, (Baltimore: Genealogical Publishing Co., Inc., 1988, 920 pages), an identification of over 50,000 individuals transported from England to the Virginia and Maryland colonies as indentured servants. This book incorporates many of the same emigrants listed in Coldham's earlier works.

● Coldham, Peter Wilson, *Supplement to The Complete Book of Emigrants, 1614-1775,* (Baltimore: Genealogical Publishing Co., Inc., 1992, 86 pages).

● Coldham, Peter Wilson, *The Complete Book of Emigrants, 1661-1699,* Vol. 2, (Baltimore: Genealogical Publishing Co., Inc., 1990, 894 pages). This volume adds 30,000 emigrants.

● Coldham, Peter Wilson, *The Complete Book of Emigrants, 1700-1750,* Vol. 3, (Baltimore: Genealogical Publishing Co., Inc., 1992, 748 pages). This volume adds 25,000 emigrants.

● Coldham, Peter Wilson, *The Complete Book of Emigrants, 1751-1779,* Vol. 4, (Baltimore: Genealogical Publishing Co., Inc., 1993, 358 pages).

● Currer-Briggs, Noel, *English Adventurers and Virginia Settlers. The Coordinated Use of Seventeenth Century British and American Records by Genealogists,* 3 volumes, (London: Phillimore, 1969).

● Skordas, Gust, *Early Settlers of Maryland: An Index to Names of Immigrants Compiled from Records of Land Patents, 1633-1680, in the Hall of Records, Annapolis, Maryland.* (Baltimore: Genealogical Publishing Co., Inc., reprinted 1968, 1995, 525 pages). This index lists over 25,000 names and sources from the earliest records of Maryland. The names were extracted from colonial land patents. These records often included evidence of transportation to the Chesapeake due to the "headgrants" involved in moving indentured servants from England to the Maryland plantations. Although their English homes are not usually given, most of the persons indexed were born in the southwestern portion of England. The headgrant system ended in Maryland in 1680.

● Coldham, Peter W., *Settlers of Maryland, 1679-1700,* (Baltimore: Genealogical Publishing Co., Inc., 1995, 228 pages). This is a continuation of the Skordas book, listing names of patentees (buyers of land, or persons granted land) from Maryland court records. An early Maryland land owner was required to register the name of his plantation, and this book indexes the named plantations of early Maryland. The names of tracts often reflected a person's link to an English home.

● Coldham, Peter W., *Settlers of Maryland, 1700-1730,* (Baltimore: Genealogical Publishing Co., Inc., 1995, 228 pages). This book adds 3,500 names.

● Coldham, Peter W., *Settlers of Maryland, 1731-1750,* (Baltimore: Genealogical Publishing Co., Inc., 1995, 306 pages).

● Coldham, Peter W., *Settlers of Maryland, 1751-1765,* (Baltimore: Genealogical Publishing Co., Inc., 1995, 228 pages).

● Coldham, Peter W., *Settlers of Maryland, 1766-1783,* (Baltimore: Genealogical Publishing Co., Inc., 1995, 204 pages). This lastest book adds 4,500 names to the colonial Maryland settlers list. All Coldham books are available from AGLL Genealogical Services, PO Box 239, Bountiful, UT 84011.

● Ferris, Benjamin, *A History of the Original Settlements on the Delaware, From its Discovery by Hudson to the Colonization under William Penn: to Which is Added an Account of the Ecclesiastical Affairs of the Swedish Settlers, and a History of Wilmington, From its First Settlement to the Present Time,* (Wilmington, DE: Wilson & Heald, 1846, 312 pages).

● Myers, Albert C., *Quaker Arrivals at Philadelphia, 1682-1750,* (Baltimore: Genealogical Publishing Co., Inc.).

● Myers, Albert C., *Immigration of the Irish Quakers into Pennsylvania, 1682-1750: With Their Early History in Ireland.* (Swathmore, PA: A.C. Myers, 1902, reprinted 1966, 477 pages. Available at the Family History Library in Salt Lake City).

● O'Brien, Michael J., *The Irish in America: Immigration, Land, Probate, Administrations, Birth, Marriage, and Burial Records of the Irish in America in and About the Eighteenth Century,* (Baltimore: Genealogical Publishing Co., Inc., 1965, 63 pages).

● Dobson, David, *Directory of Scottish Settlers in North America, 1625-1825,* Vol. 1. From ship's passenger lists, 5,000 Scottish emigrants are identified. Publ. 1984, 1988, 267 pages. (Available for $23.50 from AGLL Genalogical Services, PO Box 329, Bountiful, UT 84011).

● Dobson, David, *Directory of Scottish Settlers in North America, 1625-1825, Vol. 2.* From printed sources, 4,000 Scottish emigrants are identified. Publ. 1984, 1993, 216 pages. (Available for $23.50 from AGLL Genalogical Services, PO Box 329, Bountiful, UT 84011).

● Dobson, David, *Directory of Scottish Settlers in North America, 1625-1825, Vol. 3.* From newspapers, 3,000 Scottish emigrants are identified. Publ. 1984, 194 pages. (Available for $21.00 from AGLL Genalogical Services, PO Box 329, Bountiful, UT 84011).

● Dobson, David, *Directory of Scottish Settlers in North America, 1625-1825, Vol. 4.* From Services of Heirs and Testaments in Edinburgh. Publ. 1985, 161 pages. (Available for $21.00 from AGLL Genalogical Services, PO Box 329, Bountiful, UT 84011).

● Dobson, David, *Directory of Scottish Settlers in North America, 1625-1825, Vol. 5.* From Canadian and U.S. Archives. Publ. 1985, 312 pages. (Available for $23.50 from AGLL Genalogical Services, PO Box 329, Bountiful, UT 84011).

● Dobson, David, *Directory of Scottish Settlers in North America, 1625-1825, Vol. 6.* From Registers of Deeds in Edinburgh. Publ. 1986, 126 pages. (Available for $18.50 from AGLL Genalogical Services, PO Box 329, Bountiful, UT 84011).

● Dobson, David, *Directory of Scottish Settlers in North America, 1625-1825, Vol. 7.* From church records, burgess rolls, printed books and manuscripts in Edinburgh. Publ. 1993, 121 pages. (Available for $21.00 from AGLL Genalogical Services, PO Box 329, Bountiful, UT 84011).

● Dobson, David, *The Original Scots Colonists of Early America, 1612-1783.* This book presents abstracts of all of the known records pertaining to the 150,000 original Scots who emigrated to the American colonies before the Revolutionary War. Publ. 1989, 370 pages. (Available for $32.00 from AGLL Genalogical Services, PO Box 329, UT 84011).

● Dobson, David, *Scots on the Chesapeake, 1607-1830,* (Baltimore: Genealgical Publishing Co., Inc., 1992, 169 pages).

● Filby, William P., *Passenger and Immigrations Lists Bibliography,* (Detroit: Gale Research, 1988). This is a list of name lists included in Filby's series *Passenger and Immigrations Lists,* in several volumes. The Passenger and Immigrations series is available in larger U.S. libraries. It combines the names of immigrants to America from more than 1,000 published lists, including many thousands of immigrants to America from Great Britain during the colonial period.

✦ ✦ ✦ ✦ ✦ ✦

Index